terra
BRITANNICA

terra
BRITANNICA

A celebration of earthen structures
in Great Britain and Ireland

EDITED BY JOHN HURD AND BEN GOURLEY

ICOMOS/UK
Earth Structures Committee

ENGLISH HERITAGE

First published by James & James (Science Publishers) Ltd, 35-37 William Road, London NW1 3ER, UK

A catalogue record for this book is available from the British Library

ISBN 1 902916 13 1

Printed in the UK by Alden Press Ltd, Osney Mead, Oxford

Disclaimer

Unless otherwise stated, the conservation treatments and repair methodologies reported in this volume are not intended as specifications for remedial work. English Heritage, its agents and publisher cannot be held responsible for any misuse or misapplication of information contained in this publication.

The inclusion of the name of any company, group or individual, or of any product or service in this publication should not be regarded as either a recommendation or endorsement by English Heritage or its agents.

Accuracy of information

While every effort has been made to ensure faithful reproduction of the original or amended text from authors in this volume, English Heritage and the publisher accept no responsibility for the accuracy of the data produced in or omitted from this publication.

Front cover (from left to right): Cottage at Lower Tribcome, near Honiton, Devon (Kevin McCabe); Silbury Hill, Avebury, Wiltshire (NMR © Crown copyright); Wychert House, Haddenham, Buckinghamshire. Back cover: Beech Farm House, Lincolnshire (John Hurd).

Contents

Foreword

The early twentieth century study of earth buildings in Great Britain and Ireland can be characterized by the research of individual enthusiasts. In 1919 the architect Clough Williams-Ellis published *Building in Cob, Pisé, Chalk and Clay* and in the 1920s the Building Research Board addressed the material. Latterly the works of John McCann and Gordon Pearson have continued the theme of individual study of this vernacular technique.

More recently, the questions of 'mapping' and assessing 'what we have' in terms of surviving earth structures in Britain and Ireland have been the province of small and mostly unpublished local interest groups.

The Devon Earth Building Association (DEBA), one of the largest three regional earth building groups, formalized its work and became an association in 1991. This led the way for others such as the East Anglian (EARTHA) and the East Midlands (EMESS) regional groups.

In 1992 networking began between the groups and national bodies under the banner of ICOMOS UK. With the support of Francis Golding and latterly, Dr Philip Whitbourn as ICOMOS UK secretaries, the ICOMOS UK Earth Structures technical committee was created. Individual focus has gradually been strengthened by group identity for the subject.

As we enter a new century, Britain and Ireland can boast a network of active local knowledge and advocacy for earthen structures. This book and the Terra 2000 conference mark the culmination of the bringing together of diverse aspects within the field. Both within the UK and worldwide, the study of the material can be said to have 'come of age' with the sharing of knowledge in a consistent, co-ordinated and co-operative way. The two *Out of Earth* conferences organized by the University of Plymouth School of Architecture (first held in 1994 and assisted by English Heritage) and now *Terra 2000* mark how far the subject has come.

Pearson's *Conservation of Clay and Chalk Buildings* (1992), Historic Scotland's *Technical Advice Notes 5 and 6* (Walker 1996) on the subject of earth structures, the recently produced *Conservation of Earth Structures* (Warren, 1999) and *English Heritage Research Transactions Volume 3* (Harrison 1999) are all recent publications which demonstrate the attention the field now commands.

Raising awareness remains a key focus. While picturesque cottages and imposing barns may have a high profile in some parts of the country, much remains hidden. Prehistoric and medieval earthworks are easily overlooked in the verdant countryside of these islands, and earth buildings are often literally hidden behind renders or later refacing. A wealth of structures with earth in their construction also remain unrecognized. Earth was utilized in mortars and finishes for thousands of stone buildings, and in earth daub of the infill panels of timber-framed buildings.

With increasing awareness of earth structures comes the need to define conservation requirements and to work towards best repair practice. There is also a need to ensure that the skills and knowledge of today's practitioners are passed on to future generations.

Earth has a future as a building material in Great Britain and Ireland. With a growth in understanding of the material and techniques for its use, it is inevitable that links are forming between conservation practitioners and those addressing issues of sustainability. Earth as a practical and viable construction material and method becomes increasingly relevant. The continuing use of earth as a building material shows the versatility of the material in its various forms.

The arrival of this book marks a successful and important collaboration with colleagues in Scotland, Wales and Ireland, who celebrate the range and diversity of earthen structures and explore the characteristics resulting from the nature of the material and the way these characteristics are employed in the regional construction techniques.

English Heritage is pleased to have been able to assist the ICOMOS UK Earth Structures Committee in the publication of this book.

John Fidler
Head of Building Conservation and Research
English Heritage
April 2000

Preface

Since earth is the world's most accessible building material, it is perhaps not surprising that one-third of the world's population lives in structures made with unfired clay subsoil; this proportion was certainly greater in the past. Historically, earth has been used in a bewildering range of building typologies, from the Great Wall of China, to a humble bus shelter in Devon, and from vast abandoned cities in Central Asia, to the graceful dwellings of the Dogon people in Africa.

In the United Kingdom, earth has played a similar role; from the earliest mound-building people through most of our history, earth structures of one sort or another were in all probability the dominant type.

Earth construction is by no means a craft of the past. In recent decades interest has reawakened as part of the global search for a more sustainable future in construction, and new generations of earth builders are appearing. Altogether the outlook is hopeful for earth construction around the world. To a great extent, information and understanding of the basic principles of the material have grown out of investigations in pursuit of best practice in the conservation of historic and archaeological examples.

This book was largely born out of this positive movement. From the outset, our goal was an assessment of the current state of earth building in all parts of the UK. The authors have sought to explore where earth buildings are and why, how numerous they are, and in what types they occur. They have set out to examine the extent to which survivals are protected and to explore new directions for the material.

It is estimated that in the British Isles at present, some half a million inhabited earth buildings survive, in a varied range of architectural types and construction materials, each with their individual performance characteristics, regional significance and distinct uses. Earth structures survive in many regions of the UK, from the islands of Scotland to Land's End. This surviving built heritage is augmented by a large number of archaeological sites, which range equally widely, from monumental earthworks to the individual structures of abandoned historic villages.

This book is the result of a remarkable co-operation between 16 co-authors, all members of the ICOMOS UK Earth Structures Technical Committee. Many of the authors have, in turn, been assisted by regional experts and enthusiasts. The book is divided in to regional chapters, each of which illustrates the nature of earth building in the different regions. In each chapter the authors discuss a number of issues, including the historic and social aspects of earth construction in their region. Each region describes itself in its distinct regional accent and reflects what are felt to be the priorities in that region. We are delighted to include a chapter from a colleague in the Republic of Ireland. The three chapters which follow the individual regions focus on other aspects of earth in the UK. These include chapters on the archaeology of earth, on World Heritage Sites in Britain, and on earthen architecture in the new millennium.

The Committee was started through the energetic organization of Ray Harrison, and brought into the ICOMOS fold by John Warren, who has kindly introduced this volume; many thanks to them both. The editors are grateful to the authors who are named separately in the following pages, and also to all those who contributed to the completion of the individual chapters. This book owes much to English Heritage and it would not have come about without the support of John Fidler and Nicola Sterry; we are greatly indebted to them both. We would also like to thank Kate Pugh at ICOMOS UK for her practical help, and especially Holly Gourley in York who has played a vital role in the editing process.

A proportion of the profits of this book will go to ICOMOS UK, a registered charity.

John Hurd and Ben Gourley
March 2000

ICOMOS UK Earth Structures Committee

To contact authors

Correspondence for any of the authors can be sent to:

International Council of Monuments and Sites
UK Earth Structures Committee
10 Barley Mow Passage
London W4 4PH
UK

The Main centres of earth building in Great Britain and Ireland

Chapter 1: Introduction

JOHN WARREN FSA, RIBA, FRTPI

A celebration
    of tradition recognized
    of rediscovery and reinvention

Words
    seeking meaning in their mixing
    drawing magic from the mundane
    of arcane primeval buildings
    of deep history of generations
    of cob and clunch
    of daub and dabbins
    of cat and lump
    of clay and clom

This timelessness
    of use that stands forever
    of traditions passing down
    of beast and man and landform
    of build and rebuild onward
    through succeeding generations

This augury
    of past enfolding future
    of enduring fundamentals
    of tradition recognized
This is a celebration.

There is, in truth, some poetry in the architecture of earths – in some of it at least! This recitatif (formed during a lecture on earth building by John Hurd at the University of York) feels towards the intangible: it weaves around the abstract. It is a fragment of an idea.

The architecture of earths gathers strength. This last century has witnessed two counteracting currents already evident in the previous 100 years: the decline of the vernacular and the rise of the designed, which some might see as the decline of building and the rise of architecture. The very fact that the international committee of ICOMOS has chosen to describe its subject as earthen architecture rather than mud-brick building shows the way the subject is perceived. Vernacular building in earths has been restrained for social reasons rather than technical. The common perception of earth structures has been of an inferior material lacking durability. They have been seen as the product of poverty and shunned for that reason. The antithesis has seen earths as historically important and ecologically desirable. The study of earth building has been lifted to the high planes of university discipline and scientific practice. While the craftsman has taken up the trowel, the level and the concrete block, the surveyor supervises a JCB pressing straw into soil with its heavy rubber tread. This antithesis has imbued earth building with aesthetic qualities unmatched in any parallel form of construction.

So at the dawn of this new century we find ourselves legislating to protect, establishing understandings of historic significance, developing technologies of repair and promoting skills of specialist construction. This growing phenomenon rooted in the vernacular and promoted by the enthusiasms of individuals may mark the beginning of an era which revalues this humble and

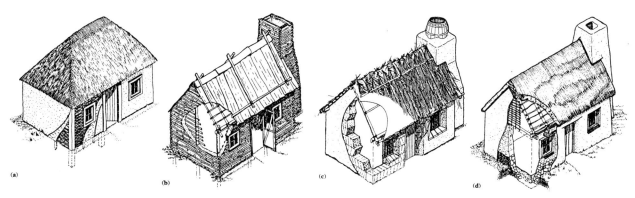

Figure 1.1. British earth building in microcosm.(a) Post frames with wattle and daub infill. Wattle and daub is typical of the south and east of England; (b) Post-fast frame infilled with mud and stud construction, found extensively in Lincolnshire. The term mud and stud, as recently applied is used for construction in which the studs are closely spaced, forming a palisade; (c) Sod construction, extensively used in Scotland and Ireland; (d) Cob construction – predominantly a west country technique. (With kind permission: Jeremy Salmond, architect).

long-serving building technology of the past and lays open important forms of construction in the future.

But the importance of this book is not that it comes at the point when the intellectual study of earth buildings has visibly, and remarkably suddenly, come of age; still less that it has come at an auspicious moment in world chronology. It is that this volume, for the first time, draws together all the threads of earth building in Britain. They are set out geographically rather than by typology but in this most down-to-earth of fields geography largely determines typology so the result is much the same.

Although small, these islands have enjoyed a disproportionate influence in the world and, unexpected as it may be at first, this influence even extends to techniques of building in earthen vernacular. At its simplest this phenomenon can be seen in the skills transmitted to British colonies and I am delighted to reproduce again through the kindness of Jeremy Salmond, architect, very telling drawings from his book Old New Zealand House, which, for very obvious reasons, I have called elsewhere 'British Earth Building in Microcosm'.

Britain, a country apparently unlikely to possess a tradition of building in earths, proves to have a series of parallel practices of wide disparity. These spring in part from prehistoric roots, most evocatively from the multi-domed houses of Skara Brae, buried in mounds on a wide northern shore, where the earth into which they were built is piled midden, now defended by concrete walls against the thrashing breakers of the Atlantic. On more sheltered southern uplands stand the multiple rings of hilltop fortifications green on their chalkland heights, and the humps of massive tumuli scattered across wide downs honouring and enclosing the distant dead. The Romans built here in their solid earthen lump and in the north threw up their earthern ramparts against the excluded Scot. Medieval man plastered his wicker huts with clay, earth and turf and then more lastingly daubed wattle panels in the robust oak frames of his houses. Through the tradition from beginning to end, solid earth walling runs

like a thread, to be supplemented finally by building in lump and pounded earth.

Although Britain, with its racial and geological complexity has produced widely varied types of earth construction, in volumetric terms this tradition has been overshadowed by the richnesses of other cultures. Climate too has obscured the tradition. Slate-grey skies, sleet, snow and winter-driven rain are with good reason a British image and it is inevitable that the vulnerability of soils has led to their protection and hence to their camouflage. Often this obscurity has left them unrecognized. Under its annual whitewash the cob cottage concealed its mud core. Whitewash also covered the daubed panels of the timber framed house. The more disciplined shapes of clay lump in East Anglia have presented brick facing, lime pargetting and tar to the outside world belying their loam and pebble cores. Equally, for climatic reasons, the proportion of earth buildings built in Britain has been much smaller than it has in the drier belts of climate that encircle the globe. So it is that the use of earths in Britain has been less evident and has represented a smaller proportion of the historic output of buildings.

The future too looks miniscule in volume but high in inventive content. Motivated neither by yearning for the tradition of earth construction, nor held back by scarcity of resources, the British building industry goes its glad way unmoved by the opportunities offered by earths. Only ecologically is there a vital spark – a glowing ember that may reignite at the flame! And it will take no little blowing on that ember to engender a viable industry in earth building in the near future. In the longer term, under ecological incentives, the picture may be very different. As will be seen in the chapters that follow, most efforts at present go towards conserving the residue of the vernacular tradition embedded quietly in the rich corpus of historic building in Britain.

Against this background the multi-authored record in these pages is to be celebrated as placing on our shelves for the first time a comprehensive survey and full analysis of the earth structures of Great Britain –Terra Britannica.

Chapter 2: Wales

GERALLT T. NASH

Wales is a small country located on the western British seaboard. It is essentially maritime in character with the prevailing onshore westerly and south-westerly winds dictating the general climate, though this is partly tempered by the warm Gulf Stream in the west. Measuring just 20,763 square kilometres, the country is dominated by an extensive upland core which increases in height towards the north-west to form Eryri (the Snowdonia mountain range) which includes Yr Wyddfa (Mount Snowdon) the highest peak in England and Wales. The lowlands are concentrated along the eastern border with England, along the southern and northern coastal belts, including Ynys Môn (the Isle of Anglesey), and in a relatively narrow band along the west coast, extending inland along the many river valleys.

Despite being linked politically to England since the Acts of Union of 1536 and 1542, Wales has its own distinct culture and language which, though in decline since the early twentieth century, is now undergoing a revival, especially in the more heavily populated south-east of the country.

Wales' economy was, traditionally, based on agriculture. The country's suitability for sheep rearing gave rise, by the Middle Ages, to a flourishing trade in wool and, in turn, to cloth manufacture and fulling. Dairying was also important, especially in meeting the demands arising from the huge growth in population during and after the late eighteenth century. Coincidentally, this was also the time that Wales was emerging as a major industrial centre, based primarily on iron, coal, copper and later tinplate and steel in the south, and slate in the north-west. By the present day, with the exception of steel, the old heavy industries have largely been replaced by electronics (Wales' largest employer), tourism and a whole range of manufacturing and service industries.

Geologically, Wales is quite a complex region, having a variety of igneous outcrops, granites, slate and more recent limestones, sandstones and shales. The stratification tends to run north-east to south-west over most of the country, but modified to east-west in the north and south. Extensive coal measures underlie the more recent sandstones, extending along the length of south Wales and, to a lesser extent, in north-east Wales, and these laid the foundation for the country's prosperity in the nineteenth century. There are also areas of soft shales, mudstones and clays, often exposed where rivers or streams have cut through overlying soils. These clays range in composition, elasticity and colour from the relatively dry, reddish clays associated with the southern and eastern parts of Wales (generally areas of red sandstone), to the sticky, greyish alluvial clays of the coastal estuaries, and the commonest type, the yellow, shaley clays found especially in the west. All these clays could be used for building purposes, though in practice the yellow or red clays were preferred.

Extensive remains of coastal promontory and hilltop earthworks, and the presence of scores of Neolithic *cromlechi* (burial chambers), show that earth has been used as a constructional material in Wales for well over 4,000 years. Protective earth-built ramparts were to be found enclosing many Iron and Bronze Age settlements, while clay was used to daub the wattled walls of many of the circular houses inside. There is documentary evidence for the use of earth as a walling material during the Middle Ages; for instance, an Inventory of the Bishop of St. Davids (1326) records that the walls of the mill at Newton in Pembrokeshire were built of 'stone or clay', while the mill at Lamphey in the same county had mud walls and was thatched.

BUILDING TYPES AND CONSTRUCTION

Floors, mortars and renders

The Welsh word for earth, *pridd*, can mean either soil, as in arable farmland or a garden, or, when used in the context of a building, invariably clay or a clayey, sticky soil which could be used for binding stones, daubing wattle-work or for making walls.

Earth was used in a number of ways in Welsh buildings. It was almost universal as a flooring material, and up to the middle of the nineteenth century nearly all cottages and smaller houses had floors of beaten earth. These were made of a mixture of clay, soil and sometimes lime or, in the case of some houses located near the coast on the Gower peninsula, crushed sea-shells. Other ingredients might include ashes or ox-blood. The increased use of flagstones or slate slabs or, later, mass-produced fired-clay floor tiles gradually made most earth floors redundant.

Clay was also used as a wall covering. When used in timber-framed buildings as a daub, or in stone buildings as a plaster, it could be mixed with cow-hair or straw to help it bind together better. It was important to ensure that the mix was not too clay-strong otherwise there would be a tendency for it to crack and disintegrate. Panels in timber-framed buildings were usually in-filled with a wattle-work of hazel. Internal partitions were also covered with clay, and occasionally bramble or even straw (held in position by thin laths nailed to a timber framework) were sometimes used instead of hazel, especially in the houses of the poor.

Figure 2.1. Clom-walled cottage near Cei Newydd (New Quay), in west Wales. The use of straw rope for securing the thatch at the gables, eaves and ridge was a characteristic feature of the area. A wooden box replaces the original wattle and daub stack. Photographed c.1910.

Stone-built houses made use of clay as a bonding agent. In west Wales, the traditional means of binding stones together to make a wall was by using a mortar made of *pridd melyn* (yellow clay) and lime. The two ingredients were kneaded together without the addition of water, relying on the moisture in the clay itself to provide plasticity.

A few buildings were erected of earth blocks or turf, but such structures were mostly of a temporary nature. These were usually *tai unnos* (one-night houses) or squatters' cabins, and were built by people desperate to secure a foothold on the common land and to claim the right to erect more permanent dwellings there.

Clom

Mass-walling, using earth, known as *clom* in west Wales, and referred to simply as *mwd* (literally, mud) in the north, was a technique used in parts of Wales up until the mid nineteenth century. It was invariably a second choice material, used where more convenient and, arguably, more durable materials such as stone or oak timber were not generally available or were too expensive. Earth-built dwellings were, therefore, associated with poorer rural dwellers: farm labourers, small-holders, estate workers; people who could not afford to buy good building stone, timber or slate. In fact, earth-built houses were built almost exclusively by, and for, the poorer members of the community (Fig 2.1).

The largest concentrations of such cottages were to be found in south-west Wales (Pembrokeshire, Carmarthenshire and Ceredigion) and in the Llyn peninsula in north-west Wales (Fig 2.2). However, isolated survivals and place-names show that they were once much more widespread. For instance, the south Wales industrial town of Pontypridd takes its name from the bridge (*pont*) by the earth house (*ty pridd*).

The clom itself could contain a variety of ingredients, but the most important was clay. This was the material which cemented the others together to form a concrete-

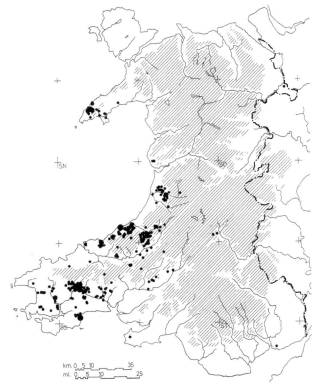

Figure 2.2. Map showing distribution of clom-walled buildings in Wales, surviving or recorded during the twentieth century. The original distribution would, undoubtedly, have been more widespread, but the main concentrations would have been similar to those shown here.

Figure 2.3. Nant Wallter, a clom-walled cottage from Taliaris, south-west Wales, built about 1780 with adjoining cow byre added about 1850. Photographed c.1900. The roof-lights are an unusual feature which were added when the cottage was lofted during the nineteenth century. The cottage has now been rebuilt at the Museum of Welsh Life, St Fagans, Cardiff.

like mixture that would form a free-standing structural element in its own right. The recipes for clom varied slightly from area to area. Sometimes, as at Llandysilio, Pembrokeshire, small stones or shale were added. Elsewhere, the proportion of clay in the soil might be less, so little or no additional aggregate would be needed. The clay generally accounted for about 30% of the mix, the remainder being made up of medium to fine aggregates such as stone dust or sand. The clom could be mixed by foot, using clogs, or horses or oxen could be employed for the task.

Chopped wheat straw was usually added to the mix to help bind the clom, though chaff, rushes, bracken and even moss and animal hair were used in some areas. The clom was mixed to the consistency of a thick paste and was then laid directly onto a low plinth or foundation wall of stone. This prevented the more vulnerable clom from coming into direct contact with the ground and the effects of ground water which might otherwise be leached up into the wall causing it to decay and disintegrate. According to local lore, the best time for erecting a clom house was when the swallow made its nest, when the days were long and the sun warm to help dry and harden the clay.

The clom was laid in layers of between 100 mm and 200 mm thickness; a three-pronged fork being the tool commonly used for this task. Each layer was allowed to dry before the next one was laid on top. It could take several weeks for each layer to dry out sufficiently for the next layer to be added. Once the walls had been built to their desired height, they were trimmed smooth using a spade or flat-headed pick. The outside walls of clom houses characteristically taper up from the foundation or stone plinth and the corners are often rounded. The internal wall surfaces were usually coated with a thin clay

plaster, while the outer surfaces were generally rendered over with a clay-based render. The walls, both inside and out, were then limewashed, an activity that was repeated annually, usually in the spring (Fig 2.3).

The clom cottages of south-west Wales are characterized by the use of scarfed or jointed crucks to support the

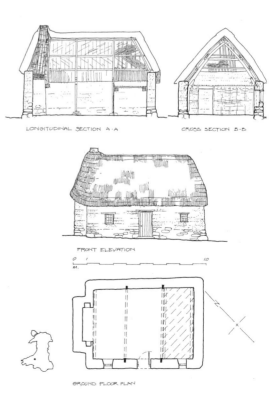

Figure 2.4. Plan, elevation and section of Nant Wallter (see Fig 2.3), as built originally, c.1780, and as rebuilt at the Museum of Welsh Life.

Figure 2.6. A small, abandoned clom-built cottage near Cribyn, Ceredigion, prior to its demolition in 1983. Areas of clom can be seen above the window and door openings where the limewash has fallen away. The thatch, including the wattled chimney stack, has been covered with corrugated iron sheeting.

Figure 2.5. Interior view of the wattled canopy over the fireplace of Nant Wallter prior to daubing with clay. The original smoke-blackened purlin supports and rafter poles are clearly visible.

roof (Fig 2.4). The cottages found in north-west Wales, on the other hand, had simple A-frame trusses that were borne on top of the walls. The roofs themselves were often quite crudely fashioned from saplings and poles resting on the purlins, sometimes forming a wattled base upon which would be laid an under-thatch of gorse, heather or bracken. The thatch, of wheat straw, rushes or reeds, was built on top of this. In Llyn, some roofs were covered in slate if there were outcrops or quarries nearby, or if waste or reject slates could be obtained at minimal cost.

Another characteristic feature of clom cottages in south-west Wales was the almost universal use of wattled chimney canopies above the fireplace (Fig 2.5). The smoke emerged through a basketwork chimney pot around which the thatched roof was formed. It was important to maintain the thatch in good condition and to ensure that no water seeped through into the wall-top as this would soon cause the wall to deteriorate and ultimately collapse. Protective measures such as slate hanging were sometimes used to protect clom walls against weathering.

THE SITUATION IN WALES TODAY

The number of clom cottages has declined quite markedly so that today there are probably just a few dozen left in Llyn and maybe a hundred or so left in the south-west

(Fig 2.6). House owners wishing to carry out repair works or alterations to clom buildings often face problems from Building Control officers who, invariably, quote sections of the Building Regulations, which appear to cast doubts as to the structural and damp-resistant qualities of such structures.

In 1990, Nant Wallter, a clom-walled cottage from Taliaris in south-west Wales, was dismantled and re-erected at the Museum of Welsh Life, near Cardiff (Plates 2.1, 2.2 and 2.3). The rebuilding of this cottage in 1992 enabled a scientific and practical analysis to be made of the methods employed in constructing such a building. This was probably the first time in a century and a half that a clom building had been erected in Wales. The publicity received by the project in the press and on television served to highlight the plight of earth-walled houses in Wales, and several house owners sought advice on how to make clom in order to carry out repairs on their own properties.

In recent years Cadw, the government agency charged with identifying important buildings in Wales, has started listing good surviving examples of clom cottages. But more needs to be done to raise the level of awareness among local authorities and individuals of the importance of these vernacular buildings, so that greater protection can be afforded to them in order to ensure their preservation and survival.

A few new earth-built structures have been erected in Wales in recent years, but these have been very small in scale. However, the internationally renowned Centre for Alternative Technology, near Machynlleth in mid Wales, is currently building a new environmental information centre and shop using rammed earth and timber framing. In another development, the winning design in a joint BBC Wales/National Museums and Galleries of Wales-sponsored competition to create a 'House for the Future' is currently being built at the Museum of Welsh Life. This state-of-the-art building, by the London-based architects Jestico & Whiles, will incorporate compressed unfired earth bricks in its construction.

Thus, for the first time in 150 years, the future does hold some hope for earth-walled structures in Wales.

Chapter 3:   The clay dabbins of the Solway Plain

Peter Messenger

THE SOLWAY PLAIN AND ITS CLAY BUILDINGS

Historically, the region has been divided by major political boundaries, the most notable of which was Hadrian's Wall, one of the area's earliest earth structures with sections constructed using the local turf. Later, the border between England and Scotland shifted up and down the region until the twelfth century when its position began to stabilize.

Physically, the Solway Firth splits the region into two contrasting topographical areas. The Scottish side is a more rugged landscape of estuaries and peninsulas created by the north-south flowing rivers and the harder igneous rocks of Criffel and elsewhere. The English side is flatter, reflecting the softer sandstones and coal measures, and there is a much wider, low-lying coastal plain that gradually rises to the higher ground of the Cumbrian Mountains. It is only at the eastern end of the Firth that the landscapes coalesce and the coastal mudflats merge into the low, gently rolling hills created by glacial erosion and deposition.

The Solway Plain has relatively few surviving clay buildings, called dabbs or dabbins, most of which are in Cumberland. They consist of domestic and agricultural buildings, the majority being of one or one and a half storeys and they are to be found around Carlisle and along the southern part of the Solway Plain westwards to Wigton and Silloth. In Dumfries and Galloway the tradition appears to be represented by a single surviving clay barn at Canonbie (Plate 3.1). The recent renovation of Burns' Cottage at Alloway exposed the original 'clay biggin' described by Robert Burns' brother Gilbert (Wilson & Chambers 1840, 98), and recent surveys have identified the existence of buildings built of clay and boul (Mercer 1997).

In Cumberland it is estimated that there are probably around 150 surviving examples[1] although others may survive disguised behind brick, stone and rendered frontages. Why so many more examples have survived in Cumberland is probably a reflection of the significant differences in cadastral and tenurial rights on each side of the border. Why, for example, in the nineteenth century, when the Earl of Mansfield wanted to build clay cottages on his Dornock and Graitney estates in Dumfriesshire, did he have to seek information from Perthshire on the method of construction (Walker & McGregor 1996, 45–8)? Had all local knowledge been lost by this time? Whatever the answers to such questions, the consequences are that far fewer clay structures have survived on the northern side of the Solway Firth. From documentary sources we can be sure that clay buildings were, at one time, far more common on both sides of the Firth and their distribution extended from the Solway to Berwick.

Most of the Solway Plain is covered by a thick layer of boulder clay which produces a pink/orange clay wall; there are also alluvial and estuarine clays which give a grey/yellow clay wall (Mosley 1978, 247). Cobble and large erratics (boulders) were available for building the massive plinths for the clay walls and the footings of the cruck frames. Clay was the most readily available material and when the labour was provided free it was the cheapest. It was also easier to build with clay than with cobble and boulders; where freestone was available (from the Carboniferous and Permo/Triassic sandstones) it was usually expensive and, frequently, of poor quality. Only a few examples survive of clay being used as a daub on wattle and the most prominent is the Guildhall, a fourteenth-century building in the centre of Carlisle.

BUILDING TYPES AND CONSTRUCTION METHODS

Even in the eighteenth century travel writers and historians viewed the method of construction as an old technique and some of them described the actual building process. For example, clay houses in the parish of Orton in Cumberland:

> are generally made up in a day or two; for, when a person wants a house, barn, etc. built, he acquaints his neighbours who will appear at the time appointed; some lay on clay, some tread it, while others are preparing straw to mix with it. By this means, building comes low and expeditious, and indeed it must be owned that they have brought the art of clay building to some perfection. They generally ground with stone about a yard high; and a house thus built will stand (it is said) 150 or 200 years (Hutchinson 1794, 515).

A similar process was described for Dornock in Dumfriesshire at the end of the eighteenth century (Sinclair 1792, 22–3). Here the 'farmhouses in general, and cottages are built of mud or clay ... These houses when plaistered and properly finished within ... are exceedingly warm and comfortable'. They first dig out a foundation trench in which 'a row or two of stones' can be laid:

> then they procure from a pit contiguous, as much clay or brick earth as is sufficient to form the walls, and having provided a quantity of straw or other litter to mix with the

Figure 3.1 Section through the wall of a clay dabbin, showing the thin layers of clay separated by thin seams of straw.

clay, upon a day appointed, the whole neighbourhood, male and female, ... assemble, each with a dung-fork, a spade or some such instrument. Some fall to working the clay or mud by mixing it with straw; others carry the materials; and 4 or 6 of the most experienced hands build, and take care of the walls. In this manner the walls of the house are finished in a few hours after which they retire to a good dinner and plenty of drink which is provided for them, where they have music and a dance, with which they conclude the evening. This they call a daubing.

By 1834, according to the New Statistical Account, the 'clay houses' in Dornock 'had almost all been pulled down, except towards the east and south-east of the parish' (Mercer 1997, 224).

The walls are usually up to 600 mm (2 feet) thick and consist of thin layers of clay mixed with chopped straw. The layers vary in thickness from 50 mm to 150 mm (2 inches to 6 inches) and each layer is separated from the other by a thin bed of straw. As the wall dried out some movement usually occurred and the layers could take on a wave-like form (Fig 3.1, Plate 3.1).

Many of these clay structures, dwellings and farm buildings alike, incorporated a framework of crucks to take the weight of the roof. They were described in the mid-nineteenth century:

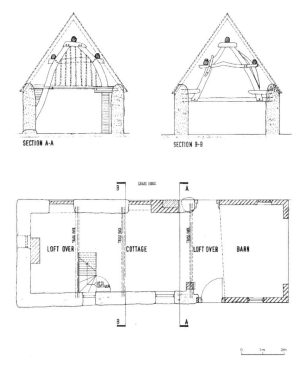

Figure 3.2. Monkhill plan and sections (John Elliot).

[T]hese timbers ... called couples ... consisted of two trees chosen with natural bends. These, when pinned together at the smaller ends, and set up in a triangular fashion ... were again fastened by a cross beam, high enough to admit of persons walking under it' (Dickinson 1852).

The pinning of the crucks at the ridge was done in a variety of ways. The most common methods were where the crucks were halved and crossed with oak pegs fixing them together; frequently the tops of the crucks were tenoned into a horizontal saddle. A rarer method, found, for example, at Baldwinholme in Cumberland, consisted of the two cruck blades being joined by a short tie beam, with the upper ends of the blades clasping the ridge piece which sits on the tie.

The buildings described above which were put up so quickly probably only consisted of one or two single storey rooms, the walls being only 2 m (6 to 7 feet) in height. A few of these have survived to be recorded, such as that illustrated here (Fig 3.2), the cottage at Monkhill, which has a dated brick extension of 1751. Most of the surviving clay dwellings have been altered and extended, adding new rooms and extra floors. Increasing the height of the walls was sometimes done in clay but more frequently this was achieved using brick or stone. There are some examples that were clearly of two storeys from the beginning and the crucks would be set higher up the wall to provide this accommodation. Occasionally the windows would have no internal lintels, having been cut straight out of the clay, and relied on the cohesion and strength of the clay wall to support the weight above.

The two-room cottage consisted of a firehouse or houseplace and parlour (or bower). The firehouse (Fig

Figure 3.3. The inglenook, heck and mell passage leading to the cross-passage. A cruck-framed clay dabbin at Rattan Row, Durdar, Carlisle.

Figure 3.4. Rattan Row, Durdar, Carlisle. The stone-lined lintel over the entrance to the cross-passage dates the extension, in stone, to the original clay dabbin.

3.3) would be the only heated room with a large inglenook fireplace next to which would be a passage (the mell) leading to a door in the gable. If an additional room was needed, a roofed over passage was created (called the hallen or throogang) at the back of the inglenook. The new room, the downhouse, would be built off this passage and could be a service room or even a low byre or barn (Fig 3.4). The three-room cross-passage plan is one of the most common vernacular forms in the region and an example from Thursby is illustrated here (Fig 3.5). Orchard Cottage also has the typical lean-to extension at the rear, often formed by a cat-slide roof. The extra space was used to provide small rooms for a dairy with its sandstone thralls or shelves. Sometimes there would be a

salting trough and another room would be used as a turfwhol or toofall which was probably used as fuel store for turf or peat.

The timber components found in the surviving clay buildings vary enormously in quality, from exceptionally fine oak of large scantling to very spindly tree trunks, occasionally with scarfed sections to make them reasonably efficient as trusses. Eventually crucks were replaced with simple tie-beam trusses, for example, the single storey clay farmhouse at High Hill, Scaleby (Fig 3.6), which is probably a late eighteenth-century structure. Many of the better timbers show evidence of reuse and there is documentary evidence to show that recycling was common practice. In those structures where there is little

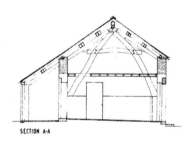
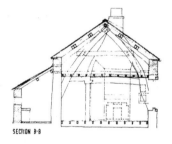

SECTION A-A

SECTION B-B

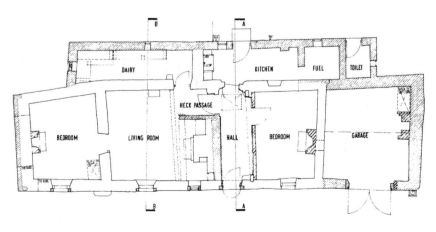

Figure 3.5. Orchard Cottage, Thursby.

Figure 3.6. High Hill, Scaleby, Carlisle. A clay dabbin with tie-beam trusses.

or no evidence of timbers having been reused or disturbed some use may be made of this fact; dendrochronological dating of those timbers may give us a reasonable indication of the age of the structure as a whole, including the clay wall.

Earlier research considered that the surviving clay buildings were not older than the mid-seventeenth century (Brunskill 1962), however recent research which has involved dating the timbers of clay buildings (Howard et al 1997) suggests that there are surviving fourteenth- and fifteenth-century clay buildings on the Solway Plain. Their age and importance will need to be re-evaluated in the light of this recent work and the strategic importance of these structures should be reassessed.

The most common vernacular material for roofing was a thatch of straw, rushes or heather. This material was laid on an underthatch of turf sods, and these were in turn laid on split rafters supported by purlins. Staples of knotted straw would be either wedged between the sods or fixed in place by wooden pegs (Fig 3.7). Some original roofs survive, albeit in a poor state, under corrugated sheeting. Without substantial grant aid none of these roofs will be repaired in the traditional manner. Where grant aid has been available in the past for the thatching of clay houses this has usually been for a reed thatch. One notable exception is Burns' Cottage at Alloway that was recently rethatched in a manner similar to that found on the Solway Plain (Fig 3.8). This shows that there are craftsmen able to do this work but at a cost and this, together with a general predisposition against thatch, are difficult obstacles to overcome. Today most of the clay structures have been re-roofed, often when an additional floor has been added, and the pitch of the roof has been altered to cope with Cumbrian slate, sandstone flags or Welsh slate.

PROTECTION AND CONSERVATION OF THE CLAY DABBIN

The re-survey of historic buildings by English Heritage in the 1980s resulted in forty-nine clay structures being listed in the Allerdale and Carlisle districts of Cumbria. Since then at least five of these have been demolished. Two or three have been added to the list in the last few years as a result of recent survey work in Cumbria. Although no new clay dabbins have been identified on the Scottish side of the border detailed research at parish level is providing us with information on demolished or ruinous examples (Mercer 1997, 224). Whatever their state of preservation, detailed recording is a necessity and the work of Historic Scotland and the Royal Commission on Ancient and Historical Monuments in Scotland (RCAHMS) is helping to create this inventory with the recording of the mudwall house at Canonbie. (Walker & McGregor 1996, 50–51).

Figure 3.7. The clay wallhead showing the traditional turf and straw.

Figure 3.8. Traditional turf and straw roof covering being laid on Burns' Cottage, Alloway, Ayr.

Figure 3.9. Moorhouse Barn, Moorhouse, Burgh by Sands, in 1988. Most of its clay walls were ruinous. Some of the cement render is still visible.

The only surviving clay structure in Canonbie is the cruck barn at Priorslynn (Plate 3.1). Despite it being a fairly basic building it is listed Grade I, presumably because it is a rare example of this form of construction in the region. Just a short distance away south of the border a similar building would struggle to be included on the statutory list at the lowest grade. Some Cumbrian buildings with eighteenth-century datestones (which usually refer to a later extension rather than the original clay structure) were excluded from the statutory list and are still not protected. The fate of one, Monkhill, is described below. Another example of a clay dabbin with such a datestone that has not been listed is the Royal Oak Inn at Moorhouse (Plate 3.2). It now has a brick frontage to an earlier clay and cruck-framed building. The brick front elevation has a date of 1742 over the central doorway. This however was not of sufficient interest to merit inclusion on the statutory list. Recent dendrochronological analysis of samples from its crucks has been dated to the fourteenth century.

The condition of the barn at Canonbie is deteriorating. One bay, on the extreme left in Plate 3.1, has already collapsed. Other cracking is evident and the roots of young trees growing against the building are undermining the stone plinth at the front.

The rate of loss of unlisted clay structures is high. An examination of the published literature on Cumbrian clay houses reveals a frequently used phrase 'demolished shortly after survey'. and this article continues the tradition. Monkhill Cottage, illustrated in Figure 3.1, was eventually demolished in 1998. Much more needs to be done to inform owners that these buildings are valuable and that with proper care and maintenance they are sound properties. Properly cared for, clay buildings are as durable as stone. When both are rendered with lime they are often indistinguishable. The downfall of so many clay

buildings has been the replacement of the infinitely superior lime render by the widespread and indiscriminate use of cement renders.

In recent years there has been some progress in repairing and rebuilding clay structures in Cumbria. By 1988 Moorhouse Barn had lost nearly 75% of its clay walls (Fig 3.9). Nevertheless most of the rest was retained and repaired in a clay/straw mix. Rat runs were filled, the wallhead was reconstituted in the traditional manner and the cobble plinth was grouted with an appropriate lime/sand mix. Similar repairs have been carried out to Dixon's Cottage, Seaville, (Plate 3.3) where half the listed clay building was allowed to disintegrate by the absentee landlord and the local authority, before a change in ownership enabled most of the remainder to be saved.

Lamonby Farm at Burgh by Sands is a Grade II★ listed building and when the gable wall of the attached barn collapsed (Figure 3.10) English Heritage and Carlisle City Council helped to fund the reconstruction using the traditional methods described above. This was a rare regional instance of twentieth-century clay building

Figure 3.10. Barn at Lamonby Farm, Burgh by Sands. The collapsed clay walls in 1993.

Figure 3.11. Barn at Lamonby Farm, Burgh by Sands. Rebuilding the clay walls.

Figure 3.12. Barn at Lamonby Farm, Burgh by Sands. The walls rebuilt in clay and straw.

construction (Figs 3.11 and 3.12). Since then, smaller clay building projects have been planned and undertaken, particularly with the help of the Construction Industry Training Board and local schools, to show that clay is still a versatile and environmentally friendly building material.

ENDNOTE

1   Current survey work being carried out by Nina Jennings is shortly to be published by the Cumberland and Westmorland Antiquarian and Archaeological Society.

NOTES

R. W. Brunskill, The clay houses of Cumberland, in *Transactions of the Ancient Monuments Society*, **10** (1962), 72.

W. Dickinson, The farming of Cumberland, in *The Journal of the Royal Agricultural Society of England*, **XIII**, Pt.II, (1852), 275.

R. Howard, et al. Nottingham University Tree Ring Dating Laboratory : Dendrochronological Survey of Clay Dabbings on the Solway Plain, in *Vernacular Architecture*, **28** (1997) 33–134.

W. Hutchinson, *The History of the County of Cumberland*, (1794).

R. Mercer, *Kirkpatrick Fleming, Dumfriesshire : An Anatomy of a Parish in South West Scotland*, (Dumfries: Dumfriesshire and Galloway Natural History and Antiquarian Society **106**, 1997).

F. Mosley (ed.), *Geology of the Lake District* (1978).

Sir J. Sinclair, *The First Statistical Account of Scotland*, (1792) **2**.

B. Walker and C. McGregor, *Earth Structures and Construction in Scotland*, Historic Scotland Technical Advice Note 6, (Historic Scotland: Edinburgh, 1996).

Wilson, and R. Chambers, *Land of Burns: A Series of Landscapes and Portraits, Illustrative of the Life and Writings of the Scottish Poet*, **1** (1840).

GLOSSARY

Bower/Parlour	Originally a principal bedroom.
Clay Dabbin, Dabbing, Daubing, Daubie, Daubin, Dabb or *Biggin*	Refers to the type of building and to the method of construction.
Downhouse	Usually a service room such as a scullery, back kitchen or brewhouse - on the opposite side of the cross-passage from the Houseplace.
Firehouse	The main heated ground floor room of a cottage or farmhouse.
Hallen	Through- or cross-passage between the Firehouse and the Downhouse.
Heck	Partition of stone or timber separating the main hearth or inglenook from the mell passage.
House/Houseplace	Alternative for the Firehouse.
Mell	Short passage adjacent to the inglenook leading into the Firehouse either from the cross-passage or the main entrance.
Thrall	Sandstone shelving.
Throogang	Cross-passage.
Turfwhol/Toofall	A lean-to extension providing various small rooms such as a dairy and for storing fuel such as peat or turf.
Sile	A cruck blade.

ACKNOWLEDGEMENTS

The author thanks Nina Jennings for providing information on many of the clay buildings in the region; John Elliott for the plans illustrated here; and Mr and Mrs Stuart Eastwood for permission to use the plan of Orchard Cottage, Thursby.

Plate 2.1. *Nant Wallter, during course of reconstruction at the Museum of Welsh Life. The first layers of clom have been laid on top of the stone foundation, and the scarfed crucks are already in place.*

Plate 2.2. *Forming the top layer of clom on one of the gable walls of Nant Wallter. The rough pole rafters are driven into the top of the walls ready for wattling.*

Plate 2.3. *Nant Wallter, a late eighteenth-century clom cottage, as reconstructed at the Museum of Welsh Life in 1993.*

Plate 3.1. *The Grade A listed barn at Priorslynn, Canonbie, Dumfries and Galloway, now in need of care and attention.*

Plate 3.2. *The Royal Oak Inn, Moorhouse, Burgh by Sands, Carlisle. The brick façade of 1742 to a clay building with fourteenth-century crucks (not listed).*

Plate 3.3. *Dixon's Cottage, Seaville, Silloth, Allerdale District. Late eighteenth-century cottage, formerly listed, but allowed to fall into disrepair*

Plate 4.1. A wychert cottage at Haddenham, Buckinghamshire, the plaster decorated with motifs of building tools in pargetted panels.

Plate 5.1. Claywall structure: Hugh Miller's cottage, Cromarty. © *B. Walker.*

Plate 4.2. Withern Cottage as found with its brick facing removed. This building was recorded and moved by Rodney Cousins to Church Farm Museum (see Fig 4.9 for result).

Plate 5.2. Wattle and daub (stake and rice) canopy chimney, Torthorwald, Dumfriesshire. © *B. Walker.*

Plate 4.3. Woodman's cottage at Harrington.

Plate 4.4. Mud and stud cottage at Butterwick, Lincolnshire in serious condition.

Plate 5.3. Neolithic houses waterproofed with clay behind the stonework, Skara Brae, Orkney. © *B. Walker.*

Plate 6.1. Garden House, West Harling. Flint faced clay-lump.

Plate 6.2. Seamere, Hinham. Wattle and daub panels being remade.

Plate 7.1. Milton Abbas, Dorset. A typical example of the late eighteenth-century semi-detached cottages in the village. The entrance lobby is shared by the two dwellings. The village was relocated so that the site of the original market town of Milton Abbas could be absorbed into the landscaped grounds of the nearby country mansion. It is not unusual to see such attempts at repair during recent decades, sadly with the loss of the original material.

Plate 6.3. Fen Lane, East Harling Render removed prior to re-rendering.

Plate 7.2. Hardy's Cottage, Higher Bockhampton, Stinsford, Dorset. Late eighteenth-century, cob walls with the front faced in brickwork. Thomas Hardy's birthplace.

Plate 8.1. Sixteenth-century cob longhouse near Holsworthy, Devon.

Plate 8.2. Eighteeenth-century cob corn barn near Crediton, Devon: the lifts show clearly.

Plate 8.3. Cob house extension at Down St Mary, Devon built in 1991–2 with its builder, Alfred Howard.

Plate 9.1 Hill of Tara, Co. Meath.© Dúchas, The Heritage Service, Dublin.

Plate 9.2 Dun Ailinne, Co. Kildare.© Dúchas, The Heritage Service, Dublin.

Chapter 4: The East Midlands

John Hurd

EARTH BUILDING IN THE EAST MIDLANDS

The East Midlands cover a large part of the central English plain and include the counties of Northamptonshire, Leicestershire, Rutland, Nottinghamshire, Derbyshire and Lincolnshire.

The great arc of Jurassic formations, extending from Dorset in the south-west to Yorkshire in the north-east, crosses through the whole region providing a rich variety of lias clays. In the east of the region are the silt lowlands of Lincolnshire, showing outcrops of gault clays, but also the northern limit of the East Anglian chalky boulder clay. In the central uplands, the Lincolnshire Wolds, are further red/brown cretaceous clays.

The region comprises the shared watershed of three great rivers, the Avon, the Welland and Trent. The Avon and Welland rise within a mile of each other near the village of Naseby in Northamptonshire. The Avon flows west into the Severn and on to the Bristol channel and the Welland flows east to the Wash. The Trent rises in the West Midlands and flows through Derbyshire and Nottinghamshire, joining the Humber which flows into the sea to the north of Lincolnshire in the north-east of the region.

The area has been a crossroads since before the Roman period. Widespread cultivation was well established, especially in Lincolnshire and Leicestershire, although in Nottinghamshire large areas of forest remained until fairly recently. Three Roman roads cross the region: Watling Street in the west, Fosse Way which cuts diagonally from south-west to north-east and Ermine Street running due north-south, isolating Lincolnshire to the east.

Given the rich selection of clays, it is perhaps not surprising that earth has been used as a structural material since the earliest times. Paleolithic sites exist in Derbyshire, but perhaps the Neolithic long barrows of Lincolnshire represent the earliest structural use of clay, with clay subsoil heaped over a wooden or turf mortuary chamber. To the west of the region, barrows are less common, but ditches, banks and other earthworks abound. Iron Age camps, Roman habitation and Saxon sites all give evidence of continuous and intensive use for over 4000 years.

There are very few standing structures of early date. In Nottinghamshire at Collingham, near Newark, an aisled timber-framed house, having small areas of surviving earth walls, dates from the fifteenth century. In Lincolnshire, Beech Farm at Greetham, having parts dendrochronologically dated to c.1400 must be one of the earliest surviving examples in the British Isles. Recently restored, Beech Farm (Fig 4.1) still retains large areas of its ancient chalky boulder clay walls.

In terms of construction methods, there is a clear division between east and west. In the west the principal

Figure 4.2. Mud and stud frame, Gunby, Lincolnshire, during restoration.

Figure 4.1. Beech Farm House, Lincolnshire, after restoration.

Figure 4.3. Hovel at Gilmorton, Leicestershire (photograph: Chris Royall).

Figure 4.5. Dovecote Flintham, Nottinghamshire, exterior as found (cracks, water damage and masonry bee).

method is 'cob', which does not vary greatly from examples elsewhere in Britain. To the east, and exclusive to Lincolnshire, is a form of cob on posts, known as 'mud and stud', where a timber frame, often of scant structure, provides an armature within the mud wall (Fig 4.2). Wattle and daub occurs throughout the region and earth plasters, renders and mortars are also common in all types of pre twentieth-century buildings.

The large variation of clay subsoils available leads to variable performance characteristics in wall quality. Perhaps the best material comes from the occasional areas of chalky boulder clay, whose large chalk inclusion make walls of great strength and low shrinkage. In the worst cases, the silty clays of Lincolnshire are often mixed with high fractions of straw to provide additional binding. The poor characteristics of these soils may in part account for the use of the slender 'stud' frames.

Throughout the region, clay buildings occur where clay is available, even in villages where stone is extensively used. It would appear that the use of earth was confined to subsidiary buildings and the homes of the poor. While this may have been true in recent centuries, older survivals demonstrate that earth was at one time used for higher status buildings, farms and even manors.

The writers of the eighteenth and early nineteenth centuries obviously saw earth buildings in significant numbers. William Cobbett describes cottages in the villages south of Leicester: 'Look at these hovels made of mud and straw; bits of glass merely stuck into the mud wall' (Cobbett 1830). Few earth buildings survive in the area now.

In 1792 John Mastin, vicar of Naseby, described his village as 'built principally with a kind of kealy [lump of congealed fat] earth, dug near it ... excellent of its kind and the best calculated for building ... walls built with this earth are exceedingly firm and strong, and, if kept dry are said to be more durable than soft stone or indifferent bricks' (Mastin 1792). He goes on to describe some walls as being over 200 years old, with lime mortar lined to look like stone, and others being given an annual coat of cow dung. Mastin's description of lime plaster with struck lines certainly adds evidence to higher status at an earlier period.

In Lincolnshire, Arthur Young in 1799 recommended mud and stud for its cheapness and durability; he proposed its suitability for the peasantry estimated that the method was about one third cheaper then brick and tile (Young 1799). It seems that much of the cost was in the numerous nails which fixed the armature together.

BUILDING TYPES AND CONSTRUCTION METHODS

Cob

The cob structures of the region spread in moderate density through Northamptonshire and Leicestershire and more sparsely into Nottinghamshire. At Ermine Street, though there are rumours of cob buildings in South Lincolnshire, the cob seems to stop abruptly.

The East Midlands stock includes agricultural buildings which range from large barns, through outbuildings to hovels, occasional dovecotes, cottages and numerous walls surrounding churchyards, farms and gardens. Walls are normally capped in thatch, or perhaps as a replacement, in tile, slate or corrugated steel. Of the few complete cob buildings that still survive, there is a fine hovel at Gilmorton (Fig 4.3) which has been recently restored. It retains a hipped thatch and the mishapen monolithic walls are now protected with a mud plaster

Figure 4.4. Dovecote at Flintham, Nottinghamshire, interior as found.

Figure 4.6. Barn at Billesden, Leicestershire, showing corner tie built into the plinth, and clay bat stitches to historic cracks.

Figure 4.7. Wattle and daub on laths.

and limewash. Another example is a large shed, on the village green at Guilsborough, with a hipped thatch held on bright orange walls derived from the local, iron rich 'kealy earth'.

The cob continues into Nottinghamshire with a beautiful cottage surviving at East Bridgeford; there are also surviving dovecotes, where nesting boxes are directly formed into the wet cob, showing evidence of 'fist prints' to the back of the boxes. One of these dovecotes at Flintham was recently conserved and incorporated into a bedroom during the conversion of some buildings associated with a public house (Figs 4.4 and 4.5).

Cob construction methods do not vary greatly from those found in the mainstream cob regions from the south-west of England to the Carse of Gowrie in Scotland. A plinth course up to about 1.5 m high and often in local stone and laid on earth mortar, with a small spread footing, is topped by lifts of cob. The lifts range from 400–500 mm high and are separated from each other by a thin layer of straw often laid crossways. This is not always the case in other regions. Recently during the repair of a cob wall at Swinford, an undamaged hen's egg was found between lifts. Presumably the egg had been laid on the straw unnoticed before being covered when the next lift was added.

Window frames are supported from extended sills and lintels and resemble those in the south-west, while wallplates are normally set on top of the final lift of cob, which does not continue up between the common rafters.

There is often a pair of rails each 2–3 m long, set half way up the plinth and returning on each side of an internal corner (Fig 4.6). These rails are pinned, often with a single trennal at the corner and built into the first lift of cob so that only the face is showing. These rails effectively tie the corner together at that level. Cob buildings are traditionally full hipped and thatched, although in some cases gables in cob or brick have been added.

One handsome little barn in a garden on a hillside in a village south of Leicester has an extraordinary feature which makes it possibly unique. The hillside on which it sits has fingers of pink lower lias clays coming through a thin strata of chalky boulder clay laid above it by glacial action. The builders took advantage of this situation by building in alternative lifts of pinky brown and white. One implication of this building is that it provides evidence that farm buildings were rarely plastered or indeed limewashed; although surviving agricultural buildings usually have multiple paint layers to the exterior they are often undecorated inside. External plasters certainly exist on cob in Nottinghamshire and on the mud and stud structures in Lincolnshire.

Wychert

In Buckinghamshire, along the northern edge of the Chiltern Hills, in a small area no more than 6 miles wide, a cob construction technique called wychert is found. Although not strictly in the East Midlands region, the technique, centred around the village of Haddenham, is worthy of mention. A good number of cottages survive (see Plate 4.1) but perhaps the most notable feature of the district is the high and winding wychert walls.

The name wychert is probably derived from 'white earth', descriptive of the decayed limestone, lime and pebbles with which the clay is mixed. When tempered with straw, it produces cob of the highest quality allowing a remarkably slender wall of around 200 mm thick, over a height of 2 m. The lifts of wychert, known locally as berries, are constructed on a plinth of fieldstones, known as grumplings, and can be raised to a height of 1 m without slumping.

While farmhouses survive from the early seventeenth century, the stock includes nineteenth-century villas, a chapel and, in the village of Winchendon, cottages built as recently as 1930.

Wattle and daub

Wattle and daub exists across the whole East Midlands region. It occurs as infill panels on timber-framed buildings, especially those dating from the sixteenth and seventeenth centuries. The wattles were usually assorted hedgewood, coppiced hazel or ash, and plaited horizontally between vertical branchwood staves (Fig 4.7). The daub appears to have been laid from both sides at once and varies in thickness from 75 mm to 180 mm. It often

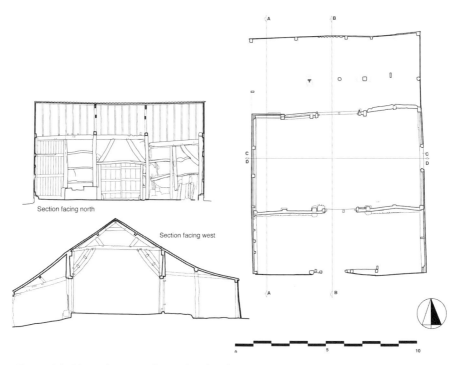

Section facing north

Section facing west

Figure 4.8. Plan and sections of a mud and stud Barn at Hagworthingham, Lincolnshire. Both agricultural and domestic buildings display the same fundamental construction methods. One unusual feature of this barn is the ladder bracing on the principal truss frame.

survives behind brick overbuilds. Newark town square is rich in old timber frames and the Old White Horse public house is a good example of the type.

In the south of Lincolnshire, Leicestershire and the county of Rutland, there is a local variation. In timber frames with close studded walls, the studs have a trench at the side of each infill panel into which slates of Collyweston stone are jammed to form a thin stone leaf. This is then plastered with mud and hay to form a secure infill panel.

Mud and stud

Lincolnshire's 'mud and stud' differs from cob in that it has a timber frame contained within the wall. It is strange that the construction techniques of earth buildings change

so completely as one crosses the border into Lincolnshire. Since Lincolnshire, especially the eastern part of the county, is off the main north-south routes, it is likely that many of its influences came by sea. While mud and stud may be unique to Lincolnshire in England, similar techniques are found on the Scottish east coast and around the North Sea coast of Holland and Scandinavia.

Thousands of Lincolnshire earth buildings had survived into the nineteenth century, including cottages, farmhouses, public houses and barns. Most have disappeared, however, due to the zeal of reformers and modernizers who regarded mud walling as degrading and insanitary. Mud and stud cottages were condemned and demolished for these reasons right up to

Figure 4.9. Withern Cottage, Lincolnshire, now in Church Farm Museum; a typical example (photo: Rodney Cousins). See also Plate 4.2.

Figure 4.10. Fulstow, Lincolnshire, historic survivals revealed after the collapse of gable end brickwork.

the early 1970s. Now only about 350 remain, of which 20 or so are close to their original condition. With a distribution almost entirely limited to Lincolnshire, the great majority of survivals are centred on the district of East Lindsey. While most of the structures date from the eighteenth century occasional buildings from the fifteenth, sixteenth and seventeenth centuries survive. (Fig 4.8)

Almost all the dwellings conform to a basic pattern, having a baffle entry onto a central brick stack, with a room to either side (Fig 4.9). Garret rooms are lit by windows in the half-hipped gables. The upper rooms were originally accessed by ladders but these have often been replaced by steep staircases squeezed into the space behind the chimney stack, opposite the front door. In many cases an extra room has been added to one of the gable ends; these are often thought to be shops or workshops. It is suspected that where these are unheated, they may have served some function in the woollen industry, perhaps for spinning and weaving which required cold working conditions to prevent embrittling of the wool. Some buildings have lean-to rear extensions which vary in length. Extreme variations include an eight bay barn and a round house.

The frame consists of a series of often haunched upright posts, called 'studs' between two and three metres tall, held on padstones often no more than flat fieldstones. Some agricultural structures and cross walls are earth fast.

These studs form bay divisions at about two metre intervals. A low brick plinth of seven or eight courses, topped with a header course, is built between studs, with earlier plinths in stone. A fairly substantial horizontal wall plate is mortised into the top of the studs, and this in turn supports close spaced rafters which are often slender undressed poles. Jointing is primitive and usually involves a large number of nails. There are slender mid-rails, which support the windows. The rails, braces and common rafters are often no more than hedgerow wood, reflecting the poverty of woodlands in the Lincolnshire agricultural community. Riven ash wood laths are nailed to the rails vertically, with gaps of about 30 to 50 mm between. Horizontal lathing is known and is seen in heck screens at Beech Farm and in a cottage at Fulstow (Fig 4.10). Ever economical, both upper and lower laths on the mid-rail overlap and share the same nail. Sole-plates are rare, with lower laths simply jammed into the brick plinth.

Unlike wattle and daub, mud and stud walls extend to cover the whole external frame, leaving the wall plate, studs and braces exposed to a few centimetres depth on the interior. The walling mix is applied in lifts of about 500 mm, to the full thickness of 200–300 mm, thinner than the cob walls of Northamptonshire. The mud and straw mix is forced between the laths with small branchwood hooks being nailed to the studs to improve the adhesion. In general, walls are battered, corners are rounded while the doors and windows have deep curved reveals, and the surface of the mud is partially smoothed using a float.

The straw content can be variable and in the poorest subsoils can be as much as 40% by volume of the wall build. Despite the slenderness of the wall, the high straw content increases the thermal characteristics dramatically. There is usually an external over render, often just subsoil and lime and cottages generally have a two-coat internal plaster of coarse stuff often reinforced with hay, and fine stuff with cow hair.

THE STATE OF EARTH BUILDINGS IN THE EAST MIDLANDS

Earth buildings in the East Midlands have had a rough time in the twentieth century. They have been demolished in their thousands. Tied cottages were not well maintained in the eighteenth century and deteriorated in the nineteenth century, as their construction faded out in favour of brick.

The remaining few are becoming rare, with only some 1000 or so surviving within the five counties. In the east of the region, the listing situation still requires further efforts with structures such as a humble slaughterhouse lairage attached to the cob church wall at Laughton and two cob cottages in Gilmorton still unprotected. A barn in Billesden (Fig 4.11) has recently been conserved and converted into a dwelling, and generally ways are being sought to bring cob back into use.

Local councils in the west of the region have now achieved a far greater awareness of the importance of earth buildings and the need for their protection, with

Figure 4.11. Billesden barn, Leicestershire, with conversion completed (photo: Chris Royall).

Figure 4.12. A fine eighteenth-century graffiti ship on mud plaster at Grainthorpe, Lincolnshire.

efforts in Leicestershire and Northamptonshire being focused by enlightened officers at Harbough District Council, who have helped to form a local interest group, Harbough and District Earth Society (HADES).

In Nottinghamshire the situation is good, with most of the small stock listed and councils active and aware of their needs.

Where mud and stud in Lincolnshire is concerned, one third of its 350 or so surviving structures are listed, protecting all the best examples (Fig 4.12). While most of the earth stock is Grade II, a star is added for several of the cottages where special or unique features occur (for example, full earth smoke hoods, heck screens and dated examples). Occasional discoveries are made and the officers of East Lindsey District Council in whose areas most of them stand are vigilant in protection and effective in communicating the significance of the type to owners and architects.

Grant funding has become less reliable across the region, especially for Grade II★ buildings which no longer attract generous grants from English Heritage. Local councils all offer support with up to £5000 being available toward conservation projects in the best cases.

There is a local interest group for the whole region, the East Midlands Earth Structures Society (EMESS), which includes members from Harbough and which regularly meets to discuss conservation matters. Members include local architects, conservators, planners, owners and others, and the group is dedicated to raising the awareness of earth buildings in the region and encouraging best practice in conservation. Mud and stud also benefits from having been the subject of a book by Rodney Cousins, former Keeper of the Museum of Lincolnshire Life who has done much to generate interest in earthen architecture across the region.

Protection throughout the East Midlands is less good in cases where parts of a building are constructed in earth: a cross wall or a remnant of surviving material, where it has been built over in brick or plastered with cement. In these cases, since buildings tend to be less 'listable', education is the best way to encourage their protection and local interest groups are a valuable help in this activity.

Earth buildings are popular with owners throughout the region and much of the stock is well conserved and maintained. There has recently been a revival of interest in the use of earth as a building material, growing out of the search for more sustainable building materials. A Lincoln architect has achieved planning permission for a traditional mud and stud extension to an existing mud and stud cottage, and there are various plans for leading edge 'ecohouses' which use that familiar range of materials, earth, straw and wood, in different proportions and innovative ways (TLP Construction 2000, Grainthorpe, Lincolnshire).

NOTES

W. Cobbett, *Rural Rides* (London: Penguin, 1830).

Cousins R, *Lincolnshire Building in the Mud and Stud Tradition* (Heritage Lincolnshire, *forthcoming*).

J. Mastin, *Papers* (Leicester, 1792).

A. Young, *General view of architecture in the county of Lincolnshire* (Lincoln, 1799)

GLOSSARY

Battered	Tapering, becoming thinner towards the top (giving the appearance of a slight lean).
Kealy	Fatty.
Cob	Monolithic piled and cut earth wall.
Wattle	Plaited or twisted branches as plastering or daubing framework.
Heck/Heck Screen	A screen forming a passage between an entrance door and the fireplace.
Earth fast	With no plinth.
Trennal	Wooden peg 'tree-nail'.

ACKNOWLEDGEMENTS

The author thanks Rosalind Willatts of HADES for supplying information for the west of the region including sections of the text, illustrations and notes; Graham Beaumont for a Nottinghamshire illustration; Rodney Cousins for help on mud and stud; and Ben Gourley for drawings.

Chapter 5: Earth building in Scotland

BRUCE WALKER

Scotland occupies the northern part of the British Isles. Its territory extends to 78,762 km² (30,410 square miles). This is not organized in a compact mass but is heavily indented, with large river estuaries on the east and with fiord-type sea lochs in the west. There are also four separate archipelagos: two to the north and two to the west of the mainland.

GEOLOGY

For its size, Scotland has a remarkable geological diversity, which reflects a long and eventful history of rock formation.

The oldest rocks are about 3,000 million years old and are considered to have been formed very slowly and in very different parts of the world to where they are now. These rocks are known as Lewisian gneiss and have been intensely deformed, cooked and recrystallized from their original volcanic forms. They were originally formed 30° south of the equator and over the last 600 million years, through the movement known as plate tectonics, they have moved to 55-60° north. During that time they were at different depths below the earth's surface, were exposed to earthquakes, rock-folding and volcanic activity, and formed part of a mountain range now represented by the rocks of Canada, Greenland and north-west Scotland.

The Caledonian Mountains were formed 500 million years ago as two custal plates – America and Europe – converged to close the ocean that separated them. The Moinian and Dalradian sediments which had accumulated on the ocean floor were metamorphosed, that is, intensely folded and crystallized, which converted the sedimentary rocks into hard brittle schists and slates. This occurred about 16 km below the earth's surface but the overburden has since eroded. The collision of the two custal plates was so intense that a series of nappes, slides and faults resulted, the old ocean floor collapsed and older rocks overrode younger rocks, reversing the basic law of geology. The Caledonian mountain pile was further complicated as great masses of molten rock rose through the crust to cool into granite. The fault lines that are most visible today are the Great Glen between Fort William and Inverness, the Highland Boundary Fault and the Southern Upland Fault. A large rift valley formed between the latter and this filled with Old Red Sandstone to a depth of 10 km over a period of 50 million years. Similar sandstone deposits also formed in the Moray Firth, Caithness and Orkney. The Caithness and Orkney deposits were in a large lake basin and formed as flagstones. Volcanic activity also affected the Old Red Sandstones of the central rift valley.

The country was then subjected to at least three ice ages over a period of 50 million years. The main effect of glaciation was erosion, especially in the Scottish Mountains where the ice was thickest. New valleys were carved and huge rock basins were formed in the weaker sedimentary strata. Lowland areas of Scotland were masked by thick layers of glacial till.

Figure 5.1. Half-timbered structure with clay infil, Head of Westbow, Edinburgh. Drawing by James Drummond, July 1849. © Crown copyright: RCAHMS

Figure 5.2. Clay thatch over claywall, Aberdeenshire. © Trustees of the National Museums of Scotland.

The net result of this long and troubled geological history is an extraordinary variety in the geology of the country. This has had a profound effect on the scenery, which is reckoned to be amongst the most varied of any country in Europe. In terms of colour and performance characteristics, the variety of clays is as complex as the geology that formed them, and the glaciation which moved them around. This leads to an equally large range of building types and uses of clay subsoils and turf.

SCOTTISH REGIONS

The country is subdivided into four principal mainland regions and four major archipelagos.

The principal mainland regions are: the North Highlands, the Central Highlands, the Central Lowlands and the Southern Uplands. The archipelagos are: the Shetland Islands, the Orkney Islands, the Outer Hebrides and the Inner Hebrides.

The population in 1992 was 4,957,290, giving a population distribution over the entire country of 61.4 persons per km². This does not give an accurate impression, since the bulk of the population lives in the Central Lowlands, the smallest of the mainland regions, and the Central Highlands are often described as 'the last great wilderness in Europe'.

The Northern Highlands can be divided into the North-west Highlands, the Flow Country of Caithness and Sutherland (an area of blanket bog) and the Coastal Plain of Easter Ross, the Black Isle and the area round the Beauly Firth, Inverness-shire.

The Central Highlands comprise the Grampian Mountains, the coastal plain known as the Laigh of Moray, and the Banff-Buchan peninsula.

The Central Lowlands contain the three great river estuaries, the Firth of Clyde in the west and the Firths of Forth and Tay in the east. These Firths permit shipping to penetrate deep into the most fertile and industrial parts of the country.

The Southern Uplands stretch across the country to the south and from the boundary with England along the line of the Cheviot Hills. The Solway Plain extends into south-west Scotland along the north shore of the Solway Firth.

Figure 5.3. Mudwall barn and stable dating from 1784, extended in claywall during the late 19th Century, Flatfield, Errol, Perthshire. © B. Walker

The island groups are equally diverse. Shetland forms the most northerly archipelago and is considered by many people to be remote, but in the context of the Scandinavian-based civilization which extended from the Baltic to Greenland and from the North Cape to Normandy, Shetland was almost central; and Lerwick, Shetland's capital, is almost equidistant from Bergen (Norway) Torshavn (Faroe) and Aberdeen (Scotland). Shetland was part of Norway until 1469, when the King of Denmark pledged his lands in Shetland to the King of Scots in settlement of a dowry of 8,000 florins of the Rhine.

Orkney lies between Shetland and the Scottish mainland. This ring of 67 islands, of which only one-third are inhabited, has the distinction of possessing the highest concentration of prehistoric monuments to be discovered anywhere in northern Europe. This partly reflects the strategic importance of these islands, which continued during two World Wars in the twentieth century, when they were the main anchorage for the British North Atlantic Fleet controlling the passage of ships from both the Baltic and the North Sea into the North Atlantic. Between the two archipelagos, the Orkneys and Shetlands form an island chain stretching 288 km north from the coast of the Scottish mainland, and effectively separate the North Atlantic from the North Sea.

The Outer Hebrides, now known as the Western Isles, form an almost continuous chain of islands stretching over 200 km from the Butt of Lewis in the north to Barra Head in the south. They are separated from the Scottish Mainland by the Minch and have a series of outliers to the north and west of the main group. These include North Rona and Sula Sgeir to the north, and the Flannan Islands and St Kilda (now a World Heritage Site) to the west.

The Inner Hebrides lie close to the coast of the Scottish mainland and form the western fringe of the North and Central Highlands. Although they are normally considered as a single group, there is a distinct change in character between those north of the Firth of Lorne and therefore linked to the North-West Highlands and those between the Firth of Lorne and the Firth of Clyde, linked to the Central Highlands.

Generally, the country is rich in building stone, although many of these, such as gneiss, granite, quartz, schist and whinstone, are difficult to work and were therefore ignored by all but the richest inhabitants. The sandstones are of very variable quality and although used from prehistory onwards in Orkney and Caithness, where they take the form of flagstones and are very easy to quarry even with the simplest of tools, they were still the building material of the upper classes until well into the nineteenth century. As a result, earth construction in various forms remained the common building material, especially in those areas where building was a community activity rather than a job for a tradesman. Shortage of limestone to produce lime was also significant; although limestone was available in some areas, the lime produced tended to be used for agricultural purposes rather than as mortar and when used for building was restricted to the finishing trades as plasterwork or limewash, although in many areas earths were used for plasters and external renders.

Figure 5.4a. Clay and bool cottages, Urquhart, Morayshire. © B. Walker.

Figure 5.4b. Mudwall houses, High Street, Errol, Perthshire. © B. Walker.

Prehistoric monuments such as the flagstone walled houses at Knap of Howar, Papa Westray, Orkney (3500 BC), Skara Brae, Orkney (3000 BC), and various other sites – the chambered tomb at Maes Howe, Stenness, Orkney (2700 BC), Midhowe, Rousay, Orkney (3000 BC) and other smaller examples – all utilize earth as a lubricant mortar to slide the larger stones into position and clay puddle as a waterproof layer, underfoot and round the outside of the stone structure before earth is piled round, and (in the case of the tombs) over the structure. Early archaeologists did not recognize this protective layer and it is interesting to note that all the Orkney tombs excavated down to the stonework and backfilled now drip water constantly, whereas those left intact are still waterproof.

Similar tombs in other parts of Scotland were constructed in the same way but utilized timber, rather than stone, to form the chambers.

HISTORY

The Scottish nation was formed in the ninth century and struggled against domination by its wealthier southern neighbour at various times. The English appeared to gain dominance in the thirteenth century, and a series of battles known as the Wars of Independence started.

The two countries remained independent until 1603, when James VI of Scotland inherited the English crown and became James I of England. The two countries shared

Figure 5.5a and 5.5b.Kebber and mott gablet at Hill of Fearn, Ross-shire © B. Walker

a monarch but continued as separate states until 1707 when the Scots Parliament agreed to dissolve and combine with the English Parliament as the Government of Great Britain (1707–1800) and then as the United Kingdom (1800-present).

The native language of the Highlands and the Hebrides was Gaelic and that of the Northern Isles was Norn, an amalgam of Lowland Scots and Norse.

Scots law was expressly preserved by the Treaty of Union in 1707, as was the position of the Church of Scotland and the Scottish educational system. This has conserved much of the cultural identity of the country during a period when many other aspects of the culture were being Anglicized.

The Scottish economy was traditionally based on agriculture, fishing and related trades, such as textile

production. Several primitive bloomeries operated in Scotland in the late medieval period and a number of charcoal burning furnaces were constructed in the early eighteenth century, but it was not until the Carron Iron Company pioneered the process of smelting iron using coke that heavy industries began to emerge. The nineteenth century saw an expansion in coal mining, iron and steel production, heavy industry and shipbuilding, together with the mechanization of traditional trades such as textile production, and agriculture. From the mid-twentieth century there has been a decline in the heavy industries and an increase in the production of electronic components and in tourism.

BUILDING TYPES

When considering Scottish building types it is essential to look at those of the adjoining English counties and those of the trading nations. The Solway Plain has a considerable influence on south-west Scotland and most innovation in farm building design appears to stem from the Lothians or Northumberland. Ideas then appear to travel quickly up the east coast to Orkney and Shetland before moving westwards towards the Hebrides. This pattern appears to result from the sea being considered as the principal communication route. The introduction of the turnpike road system in the late eighteenth and early nineteenth centuries increased the speed of east-west communication, as did the construction of the railway network from the mid-nineteenth century.

The above-mentioned transport patterns resulted in early influences coming from northern Europe, particularly the Netherlands and Scandinavia. This changed during the eighteenth and nineteenth centuries to an English, particularly Northumbrian, influence, although this was a two-way influence with many classically-trained Scottish architects moving south to work in England.

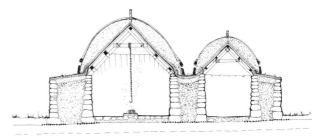

Figure 5.7. Section through stonefaced mudwall structure, 42 Arnol, Lewis. © B. Walker

Figure 5.6. Fale-walled blackhouse, c.1886, South Uist. © C. McGregor

The complex geology of Scotland and the hardness of many of the available building stones resulted in earth, in its various forms, becoming the most widely used building material from the prehistoric period to the beginning of the nineteenth century. The change from earth to stone appears to result partly from the increased prosperity resulting from the extensive markets provided by the British Empire and partly from the changes brought about by the establishment of a building industry to carry out construction works rather than building by community effort. Techniques which had proved successful for centuries were suddenly abandoned due to the labour-intensive nature of the work. Government edicts followed, stating that buildings should be constructed of 'stone and lime' or brickwork and the whole emphasis changed. This did not affect the Scottish building industry's use of earth-based mortars, and earth mortar was still being used for prestigious projects up until the First World War. By the early 1920s traditional masonry construction had given way to modern building techniques or composite construction using cement in place of either clay or lime mortars and the knowledge base began to deteriorate. This deterioration continued throughout the twentieth century and by the 1970s, when interest in the material was reawakened, there were very few clay building practitioners left to interview. Earth-walled buildings continued to be lost at an alarming rate, often with the encouragement of a bounty paid by certain local authorities on each demolition.

The need to consolidate the Historic Scotland Blackhouse at 42 Arnol, Lewis, and the subsequent purchase of a 'mudwall' and thatch school and school-house (dated to 1766) by the National Trust for Scotland provided official backing to a campaign to identify and conserve Scottish earth structures. Much has been done but, due to the complexity of the geology there is no overriding earth-building technique that can be claimed to represent the whole country and each new study only increases the range of techniques known, further complicating the task of providing sound information to conservation bodies. This means that Scotland has examples of all earth building techniques found in England apart from those involving chalk.

EARTH STRUCTURES IN SCOTLAND

Earth structures in Scotland have been classified under three main headings:

Earth sheltered structures

Earth sheltered structures include natural caves, and earth-covered structures built in all sizes. Since the evolution of the first civilizations, in almost all incidences of earth-sheltered structures, attempts were made to keep out water. The historic solution was the use of puddled clay as a waterproofing layer against the outer face of the inner structure. This is the case at early sites such as Maes Howe chambered tomb, Orkney, continuing through to modern times, such as the eighteenth-century perimeter wall at Fort George, Ardersier, Inverness-shire.

Earth with naturally occurring fibre

This category includes all forms of turf and peat construction. The largest Roman structure in Scotland, the Antonine wall, is largely built from turf. Turf and peat walls, with or without a supporting armature, and turf roofs have been identified.

Tempered earth structures

Tempered earth structures occur in a vast range, too complicated to describe in detail here. These include:

- Earth applied to an armature: this can be of stake and rice [wattle-and-daub], vertical or horizontal poles, ropes, straw mats and reeds. Typical examples include a large number of both archaeological finds and surviving structures (including a stake and rice roadway, discovered under the Marks and Spencer site in Perth).
- Construction without formwork: mudwall [cob] is the most common form of earth construction in Scotland. This type of wall can be left raw, rendered, or faced in stones or brick. Its use extends over half of the country from Dornoch in Sutherland through the coastal plain of Easter Ross, along the Laigh of Moray, through Banff, Buchan, the Mearns, Strathmore, the Carse of Gowrie, Fife and Strathearn, through central Scotland to Berwick in the east and Dumfries in the west. There are regional variations in clay character and construction methodologies, but the system is similar throughout this vast region.

Figure 5.8. Mudwall structure, School and Schoolhouse, Cottown, St Madoes, Perthshire. © *B. Walker*

- Construction using formwork: this method of construction is used to create a variety of pisé types. Wall construction may vary from simple rammed subsoil to structures containing large stones known as 'clay and bool'. Any of these can be faced in a range of materials.

As elsewhere in the UK, earth is used in a range of other techniques including plasters, renders, floors, and as a colouring medium.

Those wishing to explore further the range of techniques which occur in Scotland should consult Walker, McGregor and Little: 1996: *Earth Structures and Construction in Scotland : A guide to the recognition and conservation of earth technology in Scottish buildings.*

The wide range of earth used in Scotland made the Scots mudmasons particularly adaptable. Due to pressures at home, many of these people emigrated, taking their skills with them. Scottish-style buildings with earthen walls can be found in all the major countries that made up the former British Empire. In addition to this natural distribution, Scots mudmasons were hired by Catherine the Great of Russia to teach improved mud building techniques to representatives of all the Russian provinces. This took place in the last years of the eighteenth century and the first decade of the nineteenth century.

CONCLUSION

The select bibliography at the end of this volume indicates the scale of the documentary research, fieldwork, experimental work and conservation that has been carried out to date. This is gradually moving from the broad overview cited above, to more specific studies and case-studies of individual buildings. Historic Scotland, the National Trust for Scotland and the Highland Folk Park, Newtonmore, have been the principal contributors to date, but much more work is required to bring this useful and environmentally-friendly material back into general use. The Properties in Care section of Historic Scotland have been experimenting with the use of earth mortars to consolidate ruinous masonry structures and it is hoped to re-introduce the material into the new housing programme in the near future. Much has still to be done but, if the conservation bodies and the new-build construction industry can be brought together, we may well see a major revival of the use of this eco-friendly material.

Chapter 6: East Anglia

DIRK BOUWENS

East Anglia comprises the counties of Norfolk, Suffolk, Essex and parts of Cambridge and Hertfordshire. It is distinctive for its reclaimed marshland in the north-west with a low chalk ridge curving towards the south-west, to the east of which there is an area of blown sand called the Brecks which are approximately 1000 square kilometres. Until they were stabilized in the eighteenth century these were described as being like 'the shifting sands of the Libyan desert'. The main part of the region is the low plateau of heavy soils based on glacial deposits of chalky boulder clays which are up to 60 m thick (Fig 6.1). Towards the sea the boulder clay is overlaid with alluvial deposits and coastal sands.

Palaeolithic remains are scattered across the whole region with groups of major sites in the river valleys of the Brecks where the natural forest was thinner. Neolithic East Anglian man traded with Europe and the last land bridge with the Continent was in the north-east of the region. Neolithic flint axes have been found across the whole region, which was widely settled. Mines for ex-tracting flints for making tools occur on Weeting Heath on the Brecks. Bronze Age and Iron Age settlements occur on the chalk ridge and in the river valleys, with very little evidence of their occupation of the clay plateaus or the marshes.

During the early period of the Roman occupation the Iceni tribe, which lived in the area where buildings made of clay lump occur today, rebelled against the Romans and were defeated. The area was extensively settled during the Roman occupation and several roads were built. 'Pye' Road, which is one of the earliest of these roads, was recently found to cut through the Iron Age field pattern. This discovery that Iron Age society had enclosed fields and therefore laws, property rights and inheritance has caused historians to change their view of Iron Age society, regarding it as being more advanced than was thought in the past. Iron Age farmers produced a surplus of corn and were able to store it in holes in the ground. This surplus may have attracted the Romans to occupy the country for 500 years.

For the next 500 years immigration disrupted settled habitations and although some stone buildings were constructed, most buildings were made of wood, mud and grass: nothing of these survives. The Norman conquest in the eleventh century made the new feudal lords very rich and stone buildings in the form of churches, castles and dwellings were erected. Later, the science of carpentry improved and the structure of timber-framed houses became well thought-out. Bricks were reintro-duced in the fourteenth century, with two of the earliest examples at Caister Castle in Norfolk and Little Wenham Hall in Suffolk. This was a time of prosperity based on wool production and weaving.

Besides the few brick buildings, the majority of structures were timber framed until the end of the eighteenth century, when buildings with walls made entirely of raw earth were introduced, possibly from Spain, France or Portugal. In the first 50 years of the nineteenth century the population of England, and East Anglia, almost doubled. Improvements in agriculture provided better quantities and quality of food during the winter and the new knowledge of hygiene meant that more children survived. New farms were being built on land which had not been ploughed before. These and the large population increased the demand for building materials which were not available, so raw earth was adopted, probably by landlords at first.

East Anglia has more types of earth construction than any other region in Britain. One of these is 'clay-lumps' or, in the west of the region, 'clunch'. For about one

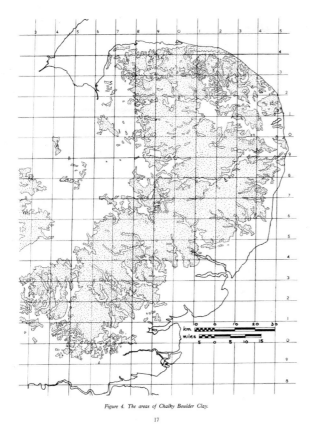

Figure 4. The areas of Chalky Boulder Clay.

17

Figure 6.1. Geological map of East Anglia showing regions of chalky boulder clay.

Figure 6.2 Old Buckenham. Clay lump houses.

Figure 6.4. London Road, Attleborough. Public housing.

hundred years clay-lump was the principal walling material for every size and type of building, almost to the exclusion of all other materials (Fig 6.2). The main reason for this was that it was cheaper than brick or flintwork. Although lime mortar was sometimes used for clay-lumps, earth mortar was more common and quite adequate. No fuel was needed in the making of clay-lumps and the main work of digging the clay could be done in the winter when there was less farm work and more labour available.

The clay lies just below the topsoil and is a mixture in varying proportions of sand and gravel, broken and ground chalk, silt and clay. Typically the clay content is about 5–15% and so the soil is ideal for making clay-lumps, mortars and renders with very little, or no, modification. The clay was usually dug where the buildings were to be built and the holes became ponds, many of which survive.

The clay was dug in winter so that the frost would break up the fragments of clay and let the water in to soften the clay. This saved a lot of work when the clay was spread out and trodden by a horse, donkey or ox to a paste. Straw, or any other available fibre, was mixed into the clay.

There are examples of buildings which have no plinths. Most walls have an underpinning of bricks and so clay-lumps are made to the dimensions of house bricks.

The most common sizes are:

• One brick, less the thickness of the external render, wide and 2 bricks long where the external render

Figure 6.3. Wilby Canal. Norwich ochre limewash.

stops at the plinth and the internal plaster goes over the plinth.
• One brick, less the thickness of the render on both sides where the internal render stops at the plinth in agricultural buildings, dairies and wash houses.

Clay lumps are usually 2 bricks long but are occasionally found to be 2.5 bricks long. Clay-lumps which are taller than 150 mm are rare.

When the lumps were made, the clay-straw paste was put into the mould and pushed into the corners. The top was struck level and the mould removed immediately and another lump made next to it. It was said that two men with prepared clay could mould 400 clay-lumps in a day. Each clay-lump used about 32 kg of wet clay. When the clay-lump was dry enough it was turned on to its edge and then on to its end before being stacked. A dry clay-lump weighed about 25 kg.

Mortar was prepared by picking out the stones from the wet clay from which the lumps are made. When made the dry lumps drew the moisture from the clay mortar almost as soon as the clay-lump is laid, so laying lumps could be continuous. If the clay-lumps had not dried sufficiently for an earth mortar to be used lime mortar could be used instead.

Earth, earth and lime and lime renders were used inside and outside and were finished with distemper paint on the inside and limewash on the outside. Pink was the favourite colour in Suffolk whereas pale brown was at one time ubiquitous in Norfolk (Fig 6.3). The production of coal gas in towns for lighting resulted in vast quantities of coal tar which was adopted for protecting the external walls of all sorts of buildings and was often used on one or more walls on dwellings. Later, better rents would be paid for clay-lump houses which had one or more elevation faced with brickwork or flintwork (Plate 6.1). Many existing clay-lump houses had brick veneers fixed to them by nailing brackets to the clay-lump which were then built into the courses of bricks at every 6–8 courses (Fig 6.4).

Lime in East Anglia is burnt from chalk and has no hydraulic set. Brickwork laid with this mortar is not very strong. Clay-lumps laid in earth mortar were as strong as brick walls and possibly stronger. Beyond this, clay-

Figure 6.5. Redhill Farm, Ovington. Cob walls to ground floor with clay-lump above.

Figure 6.7. South Farm, Hargham. Tarred shuttered clay farm buildings.

lump houses could be built in the style which was fashionable, which could not be done easily with timber-framed houses.

Two tower windmills, made with earth, were both built around 1830. The Carleton Rode windmill was six storeys tall and worked for about 75 years. Local tradition is that the miller's son was a giant and he trod the clay on the wall himself. If this is true then the windmill was probably built of cob and not clay-lump. There are isolated examples of cob which is usually identified by the wall being thinner higher up. The cob walls are relatively thin, being as little as 1.5 bricks thick. In one farmstead all the buildings have cob up to the first floor joist level with clay-lumps above (Fig 6.5). The thatched cob wall in Ashwell in Hertfordshire is a fine example.

A pisé building was discovered a few years ago at Marden Ash just north of Chipping Ongar in Essex (Fig 6.6). It is a polite building, a 'cottage orné' and is made of a gravel containing a lot of iron oxide. This building dates from 1790 and was probably built as a direct result of the pamphlets published by the Frenchman Francois Cointereau. Several such cottages were reported at the time, but this is the only one that has been found so far. There are modern pisé buildings in the region.

Peculiar to the region are buildings made of 'shuttered clay' (Fig 6.7). These are not pisé. The clay is not suitable for pisé and was clearly put into the shuttering as a paste and was sometimes pricked with sharpened sticks to provide a key for the plaster after the shuttering had been removed. These walls seem to occur only on landed estates and were used for every sort of building. It is thought that the estates could afford the cost of the shuttering and the advice of the architects and engineers. Walls can be built as little as one brick thick with this method, but skill is required with this technique in controlling the cracking and the drying so that the wall does not deform. It is clear that different, or modified, subsoil was used and that it was selected for its reduced shrinkage. Knowledge of the properties of subsoil from different areas has been lost and may never be recovered unless clays are readopted as a walling material more widely.

Timber-framed houses occur throughout the region. Some date from the thirteenth century but the form

Figure 6.6. Marsden Ash, Essex. Pisé cottage with long straw thatch.

Figure 6.8. Kingshead Cottage, Banham. Timber frame with new render and wattle and daub.

stopped being built in the late eighteenth century (Fig 6.8). They depend on an infill of 'wattle and daub' sticks and mud except where panels of brickwork have been put in instead. East Anglian timber-framed houses typically have narrow panels and studs that are one or sometimes two storeys tall. The timber frame is exposed on the outside only occasionally. Usually the houses are covered with render which traditionally was made of lime, or earth and lime, and painted with limewash. In parts of the region the outside surfaces are sometimes decorated with incised and pricked patterns known as 'pargetting'.

The spaces between the studs were traditionally infilled with thin vertical sticks tied to horizontal sticks, which were originally sprung between the studs of timber frame and in later repairs were nailed to the outer face of the studs (Plate 6.2). A paste made of subsoil and chopped straw or any other fibre and occasional additives was pressed through the sticks and spread on either side to a thickness of about 100 mm. The external render is put on to plasterers' laths nailed to the outside of the frame (Plate 6.3).

Wattle and daub is sometimes found forming ceilings and, rarely, suspended floor coverings. Earth is sometimes found as mortar for bricks in chimneys and as the lining to the flues because it is resistant to the sulphates in smoke which attack lime in mortars. Earth mortars are also used to prevent snow and rain being blown into the roof through the tiles and slates where the mortars are often put on water reeds laid between the tile battens.

The majority of earth buildings are agricultural and, on becoming redundant, will probably be lost unless alternative uses can be found for them. On the other hand clay-lump and timber-framed dwellings are usually occupied. This is because they are regarded as good security for a mortgage. This advantage has been offset by the mortgage companies insisting that houses should have damp-proof courses in floors and walls and that old renders be replaced. Cement-based renders are usually put on by builders who do not know better.

Cement render has a similar coefficient of thermal expansion as steel whereas earth walls tend to shrink when warmed as moisture evaporates. The result of this contrary movement is cracks in the render which draw in water, which accumulates and can eventually cause the wall to move.

Cement renders on ancient timber-framed houses, many of which are protected by law because of their architectural or historic interest, have an insidious effect. Moisture condensing on the inside surface of the render raises the moisture content of the timbers which provides ideal conditions for deathwatch beetles (*Xestobium rufovillosum Anobidae*) which will destroy whole timbers.

Where earth in building is being repaired, earth salvaged from the buildings should be reconstituted and replaced. Repairs to earth walls are divided into either a patch where the repair is small enough for shrinkage not to be a problem, or earth blocks cut out and fitted in earth mortar.

EARTHA, the East Anglian Earth Building Group, organises demonstrations and lectures for the public and professionals involved in inspecting and repairing buildings. Success is slow, steady and cumulative.

Very few clay-lump buildings are protected by being listed of 'architectural and historical interest' because most were built after 1840. After this date only exceptional buildings are protected. Very many timber-framed buildings, which are listed, retain their wattle and daub infill panels and now that there are more workmen who have the necessary skills to repair, restore and replace these panels, good work is being done to protect the character of these buildings.

Houses with raw earth in their construction are regarded by the companies who grant mortgages as good security and this has allowed these buildings to be occupied. EARTHA has raised awareness of the special problems of earth buildings among conservation officers, builders, plasterers and the surveyors who inspect buildings for mortgage companies. Several of these now require cement renders to be removed which makes the mortgage companies a force in conservation.

Chapter 7: Wessex

GORDON T. PEARSON AND ROBERT NOTHER

The ancient kingdom of the West Saxons has no identifiable boundaries but is thought to have encompassed Hampshire, Dorset, Wiltshire, Berkshire, Somerset and Devon. King Alfred made Winchester its capital and Thomas Hardy immortalized the kingdom in his novels, concentrating on stories of Dorset, Hampshire and South Wiltshire. It is this area which is more generally regarded today as Wessex.

Geologically, the area comprises recent rocks from the Cretaceous and Tertiary periods with chalk downland dominating the lowlands (Fig 7.1). Chalk (calcium carbonate) was the last sedimentary rock to be laid down and was formed between seventy and one hundred million years ago. It was formed in still saltwater at depths of less than two hundred metres and comprises pin-sized sea shells known as foraminifera which have been cemented together in a matrix of lime secretions called coccoliths. It was laid down in layers known as upper, middle and lower chalks, each separated by a layer of hard chalk rock. Upper chalk dominates the downland and has been used in pulverized form to construct the walls of many fine buildings due to its suitability to pisé work. The chalk belt runs from the rim of the Weald on the Hampshire/Sussex border, across central Hampshire and meets the upper greensand near Warminster (Wiltshire), taking in Salisbury Plain. A spur runs from the north-east of Dorset at its border with Hampshire and Wiltshire, westwards to beyond Dorchester.

Soils from the tertiary period overlie the chalk and were formed between one and seventy million years ago. They are acidic in nature and comprise gravels, sands, silts and clays which cover vast areas of the New Forest and the heathlands of Dorset. Man has used this material for generations to construct the walls of more humble buildings, using the piled method of construction. Where chalk, clays, sands and gravel are found in proximity, the materials were sometimes used together, such as around Bere Regis where chalk is found as an aggregate bound within clay (Fig 7.2).

Wessex is a rural area, its largest centres of population being Southampton and Portsmouth. The growth of the holiday trade around Bournemouth, Poole and south-east Dorset has given rise to much twentieth century development, with a considerable influx of retired residents. Traditionally, chalk downland was ideal for the rearing of sheep but during the last century there has been a dramatic change with 96% of it having been ploughed for the intensive cultivation of cereal crops. Apart from at their margin, the acid heathlands have largely escaped the pressures of change but

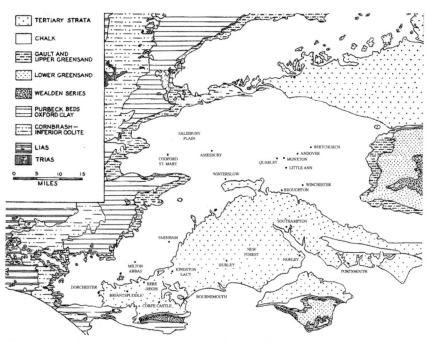

Figure 7.1. Geological map of Wessex. Earth buildings are found throughout the chalk and tertiary areas. The area is dominated by alkaline soils of the chalk downland which rise to 150 metres. The tertiary strata of the New Forest and Dorset heathlands comprise clays, sands and gravels, and are acidic.

Figure 7.2. Shitterton, Bere Regis, Dorset. This boundary wall contains two different earth mixes, one chalk-based, and one clay but with chalk particles among the aggregate. Bere Regis sits predominantly on chalk but just to the south of the village are the former heathlands with their sands, gravels and clays.

Figure 7.4. Examples of cob mixes across Dorset. The left-hand sample is from Lulworth, close to the south coast. The middle example is from Shitterton, some eight to ten miles north of Lulworth. The right hand example, almost fully chalk, is from Farnham in north-east Dorset, close to the Wiltshire and Hampshire boundaries.

large areas of the Dorset heathland have been taken for development due to pressure for housing the population following the north-south migration which still continues.

THE PILED METHOD OF CONSTRUCTION

This method of construction dominates the rural areas of western Wessex. It was used in both clay and chalk areas until about 1914 and some villages are dominated by it such as Winterslow (Wiltshire), Milton Abbas, Briantspuddle and Farnham (Dorset), and Monxton (Hants) (Plate 7.1 and Fig 7.3). The underpin foundation courses are of flint in downland areas and generally of limestone elsewhere but with brick being used commonly in later examples. Some New Forest and south-east Dorset cottages have a row of Burley sandstone boulders or, occasionally, rise from the ground without any foundations. Traditionally, the method is associated

with thatched roofed buildings, whether dwellings or agricultural structures. In some predominantly stone areas, such as Corfe Castle and various villages of south-east Dorset, clay-based piled toppings to the walls are often present (Fig 7.4). These provide a ready means of fixing the lower thatch layers over the eaves.

Gable walls are almost unknown and where found are usually of lightweight timber construction with brick infill and rendered to match the earth wall below. They would have been uneconomic to construct and prone to collapse until the roof structure had been added. However, occasional examples are found such as at Codford St Mary (Wiltshire).

Door and window openings tend to be small in relation to the overall size of a wall due to the weak nature of the material, and heavily overhung eaves protect the lime-rendered walls of the buildings or the chalk-slurried boundary walls. They were usually cut out of the earth wall following its construction, the timber lintels having

Figure 7.3. Briantspuddle, Dorset. Cob and thatched buildings contribute significantly to the distinctive character of this village and date from the fifteenth to the nineteenth centuries. Many were formerly agricultural buildings which have been converted into dwellings, and in one case, into the village hall.

Figure 7.5. Winchester, Hampshire: a good example of a rammed chalk house of the mid nineteenth century. These buildings were designed by local architects for wealthy townsfolk. Most have basements with walls of random chalk rubble. Original renders usually remain and comprise a thick, soft, lime-based render coat with a thin, hard, cement-based setting coat.

been built in as work proceeded. However, in later buildings, timber plugs were cast in during construction around openings to allow fabricated joinery to be fixed once the wall had dried out.

Most buildings were two storeys in height. In Hampshire, the wall thickness was constant although chalk walls tended to be thinner than their clay counterparts due to their greater strength. Towards the west of the region, the thick walls sometimes tapered towards the top, a feature which first appeared on the western edge of the New Forest. The storey heights tended to be very low, particularly in older buildings, the upper floor being contained partially within the attic space under a collared roof.

The idea of ramming damp earth between strong shuttering was not new when it was reintroduced to Hampshire at the end of the late eighteenth century, as pre-Roman evidence at Basing House confirms. Upper chalk was found to be ideally suited to this method of construction and by 1819, it was recorded as being in regular use in the county (Rees 1819). Containing no added water, it allowed an immediate load to be taken and needed little drying out. It was quicker to construct than the piled method of construction and became a popular method in the market towns of Hampshire during the Regency period. Many grand houses were constructed in towns such as Andover, Whitchurch and Winchester where surplus excavated chalk from the construction of the railways was used to the designs of local architects. Wall thickness was usually reduced at each floor level and window jambs were normally splayed.

The external faces of the walls were rendered using newly patented cements, and openings were accentuated with mouldings run *in situ*. A projecting band course at first floor level and a high, projecting plinth course was also usual. Many of these buildings had basements which might have been the source of the chalk in some cases. Basement walls were inevitably of fist-sized nodules of hard chalk set in a soft, lime-based mortar as random rubble.

Door and window openings were much larger than those found in buildings constructed by the traditional method due to the higher strength achieved by the ramming process which allowed cementitious renders to be used. They were formed by dropping pre-formed boxings into the shutters with timber plugs lightly attached which remained embedded in the chalk following removal of the shutters. Door and window frames were then able to be secured.

Fine buildings of rammed chalk were built to modern designs of the time for wealthy townsfolk and they dominated the best sites in rapidly expanding towns such as Winchester, where a five storey house still stands overlooking Oram's Arbour (Fig 7.5).

THE PUDDLED METHOD OF CONSTRUCTION

A hybrid method of the piled and rammed methods was used in Hampshire and probably Dorset in the middle of the nineteenth century (Fig 7.6). A blend of clay, silt, sand and gravel were mixed with straw and water and thrown into shuttering before being lightly plugged and allowed to dry. Sheltered, unrendered walls witness this method where the earth oozed through badly fitted boards and remains to this day. The extent of its use is not known as most buildings give no hint of its construction but a cottage at Fawley (Hampshire) was demolished in 1987. W. Jaggard experimented with this method of construction at Amesbury (Wiltshire) in 1920 using chalk. Of the five methods that he used for his experiments he considered that the puddled chalk walls were the most satisfactory, despite their slow progress (Jaggard 1921).

Figure 7.6. Church Villa, East Morden, Dorset. An early nineteenth-century example of a 'polite' building with cob walling. It is believed that the walls were shuttered during construction, following the puddled method.

Much of the Romsey Road area of Winchester was constructed in the 1840s using chalk from the railway cuttings. The puddled method was used to construct the walls, together with piled and rammed methods, often in conjunction with block chalk and external skins of brickwork.

THE ADOBE METHOD OF CONSTRUCTION

The use of unfired earth blocks is not common in Wessex but in the 1920s through to the 1950s experimental work was carried out in and around Quarley (Hampshire) by Jessica Albery and Mr. B. H. Nixon using pulverized chalk and water. A number of houses were constructed together with a hostel, most of which have now been demolished. However, several houses still stand, such as Middlecot, Pine Cottage and Thimble Hall, in addition to a picturesque pair of semi-detached cottages at the nearby village of Little Ann, near Andover.

The blocks were cast on site in moulds and laid in a mortar of chalk and sand to which a little cement was added. The walls were of solid construction and the size of the blocks varied from one building to another. Upon completion, the external surfaces were rendered and decorated and the cottages give the appearance of normal masonry construction.

Immediately prior to the outbreak of the Second World War in 1939, a local man patented a product he named 'Durastone'. It comprised pulverized chalk and a little moisture stabilized with lime or cement and pressed from a brick-making machine. Experimental work was halted by the hostilities and appear not to have recommenced after the war. The extent to which Durastone has been used is not known.

STATE OF CONSERVATION

There appears still to be a fairly common perception among owners, builders and others within the region that earth walling is an inferior material which is best replaced by something more substantial. Of course, as with buildings of any construction type or material, the quality of the original construction can vary. In all probability, the poor reputation of earth walling is perpetuated through inappropriate repairs causing it to fail, and the belief that its maintenance is prohibitively expensive, time-consuming and disruptive.

Fortunately, this attitude is beginning to change as the cultural value of the stock of historic buildings is increasingly recognised. Where earth buildings continue to display clear evidence of their historic form they are very likely to carry listed status. In Dorset, for example, nearly 450 of its approximately 12,000 Grade II listed structures are described as containing 'cob'. Many other listed buildings are described as having rendered walls where it is now known that in very many cases the substrate is cob. Then there are those described as having brick walls where in fact the brick is simply a facing to cob walling. Perhaps the most famous dwelling in Dorset in this category is Thomas Hardy's birthplace at Higher Bockhampton near Dorchester (Plate 7.2). Detailed studies of local areas in Dorset lead to the belief that the numbers of Grade II listed structures containing cob is several times that where the material is actually identified. To this can be added the substantial numbers of cob-walled antilage structures, which although not specifically mentioned in the listing still have statutory protection.

The detailed studies referred to above reveal that for each listed structure in Dorset which contains earth walling there are several which are not listed, and a high proportion of these are not within Conservation Areas. In all probability within Dorset there are over 5,000 earth-walled buildings, the early examples being of unshuttered piled method. A substantial number of these have no statutory protection under the Planning (Listed Buildings and Conservation Areas) Act of 1990. Many of these buildings are in the south-east of the county where suburban encroachment has absorbed the former heathlands. Originally they were dwellings for small-holders or farm labourers, and probably many were built as squatters' cottages. These modest dwellings on generously sized plots have become ready targets for redevelopment, although many survive under later phases of construction. At the other extreme there are statutorily unprotected earth structures in remote rural areas which are at risk through being redundant and falling into decay; however, there are probably relatively few of these.

Regrettably, it is not possible to save every earth structure, and efforts tend to be concentrated on those that are listed and those which contribute to the special character of Conservation Areas, in towns, villages and some other settlements. This is not to say that unlisted buildings outside Conservation Areas are overlooked. With an increasing awareness of the benefits of sustainable materials, more and more owners are being persuaded of the worthiness of retaining and repairing earth walling sensitively.

The survival of so many earth-walled examples is testimony to the durability of the material. Within this region, perhaps the most notable is Cruck Cottage at Briantspuddle, Dorset, which was built in the late fifteenth century (Fig 7.7). It remains in residential use to this day. The surviving evidence of cruck construction supports the belief that originally it was a Hall House, built probably for a yeoman farmer. Its enclosed fireplace, first-floor accommodation and dormers were probably added in the sixteenth or seventeenth centuries, with further extensions and modifications later.

While there is little doubt that the value of the material is increasingly being recognised, a number of earth wall collapses during recent years has done little to promote confidence in it. Initially, the rebuilding was carried out in blockwork or similar. This technique continues, but more and more owners, together with surveyors representing house insurers, are being pursuaded of the merits of like-for-like repairs. Where major collapses occur, perhaps extending to the full height of the ceiling, rebuilding in cob is seen as difficult because of its drying shrinkage where it adjoins the existing. The use of cob blocks in repairs has grown in Dorset, mostly in vernacular buildings on the estates of Corfe Castle and Kingston Lacy, under the stewardship of the National Trust. The knowledge gained in this process by the appointed professional agents and builders is beginning to spread more widely. While not ideal in philosophical terms, as long as local material is used in the making of blocks, perhaps it is the next best solution to a fully *in situ* repair.

Of course, it is important to establish what caused the major collapses in the first place. A number have been attributed by the engineering or surveying consultants to ground movement associated with leaking drains and water pipes. However, it is worthy of note that common to all the recent collapses has been the presence of hard impervious render and plaster coatings, and excessive dampness in the base of the walls. It is tempting to believe that the greatest threat to earth walling in occupied buildings is the continued use of such coatings.

The spalling of these hard coatings and the dampness that occurs behind them is often interpreted incorrectly as a rising damp problem. This promotes the desire to insert a damp proof course, and to view the substrate material as being of poor quality. However, the message is spreading that these hard impervious surfaces are bad for the walling and that inserting a damp proof course is unlikely to be beneficial and may well be in itself damaging.

To aid awareness of appropriate repair and maintenance and the dangers of the alternatives, several local planning authorities have issued leaflets giving technical guidance. One is being planned by the Dorset authorities, and a small portable exhibition has been displayed around the county. Also, a number of continuing professional development sessions have been devoted to the subject.

A recent building (completed late 1998) at Norden, Corfe Castle, includes cob external walling. This is a public building, funded through partnership agreements and constructed by an established local general builder. The contract was let following the normal competitive tendering process required under the Local Authority's standing orders. Previously, the successful tenderer's experience in cob had been confined to minor repairs. Unlike most traditional buildings in the area, which have some form of coating, whether a lime or mud render, limewash, or a combination of these, the cob on this new building has been left exposed. This has

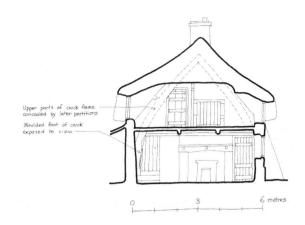

Figure 7.7. Late fifteenth-century dwelling, Briantspuddle, Dorset (illustration after Royal Commission on Historic Monuments for England). The moulded cruck frame indicates that this was a hall house of some status, built probably for a yeoman farmer. The fireplace, first floor and dormers are believed to have been added in the sixteenth or seventeenth centuries.

generated considerable interest, and the intention is that a display will be included in the building covering earth buildings and their repair.

Collectively, these initiatives appear to be helping to promote a greater awareness in the value of earth walling and how to look after it. However, there is still much to be done, and a concerted and sustained effort is needed among building conservationists to ensure that unnecessary loss of, or damage to, earth-walled buildings is avoided.

TERMINOLOGY

Buildings constructed of earth in Wessex are referred to as 'mud' buildings regardless of whether they are constructed of clay or chalk. However, the nearer one gets to the Devon border, the more one will hear the word 'cob' used. In Winterslow, where much of the village was constructed in the early years of the twentieth century, the cottages were said to have been 'swallows built', a phrase still in use in the area today. However, the nearby village of Broughton (Hampshire) refers to 'wichers' constructing walls of earth in its guide to the history of the village. In the Dorset listed building entries, whenever the substantial presence of earth walling is known, the term 'cob' is used and this now appears to be the commonly accepted term in the county.

NOTES

W. Jaggard, *Experimental Cottages. A Report on the Work of the Department at Amesbury, Wiltshire.* (London: Department of Scientific and Agricultural Research, HMSO, 1921).

A. Rees, *Cyclopedia and Universal Dictionary of Arts, Sciences and Literature* (1819).

GLOSSARY

Wichers	Builders of earth walls.
Swallow Built	The traditional or piled method of construction.
Mud	The material from which walls are constructed; either clay or chalk.

Chapter 8: Devon and Cornwall

Larry Keefe and Peter Child

HISTORICAL BACKGROUND, ROCKS AND SOILS

The south-west peninsula (Devon, Cornwall and north-west Somerset) is geologically very complex, with rock formations which yielded stone that was not always easily extracted and worked. This, together with a shortage of building sand and lime in remoter areas, perhaps partly explains the widespread use of earth for building construction in the region, especially in Devon. The geological complexity leads to an enormous variation in soils which range from heavy, impermeable clays through to gravelly sands. Consequently, although cob buildings occur throughout the region, they are more numerous in some areas than in others. By far the highest density (if the granite massifs of Dartmoor and Bodmin Moor are excluded), is to be found north of a line drawn from Torquay in the east to Padstow in the west. Within this area, in Devon and north-east Cornwall, in terms of geographical distribution and density of cob buildings, two geological mapping areas are of particular importance. These are the Upper Carboniferous (or Culm Measures) formations and those of the Permian and Triassic, known respectively as the 'dunland' and the 'redland' because of the predominant colour of their soils, which, taken together, cover around 50% of the surface area of Devon.

Within the dunland areas, the soils overlie mainly shales, siltstone and fine-grained sandstones, and are, therefore, characterized by the presence of large quantities of silt and clay, with variable amounts of sand and gravel.

They are generally buff to yellow ochre in colour. The soils of the redland area are generally less homogeneous. Soils overlying the Permian breccias may be classed as gravelly sands, while those derived from Permian sandstones contain large amounts of fine sands and silts as do the soils east of the Exe estuary overlying the Triassic sandstones and mudstones. Apart from the obvious colour difference, redland soils differ from those of the dunland in their particle size distribution characteristics, containing generally large amounts of sand and proportionately less silt and clay. Clay fractions (materials < 2 mm diameter) of 5% or less have been recorded in historic cob mixes from those areas.

Clearly, therefore, the behavioural characteristics and durability of cob walls fabricated using these widely differing soils are going to show considerable variation. This has been confirmed by recent research, carried out at the University of Plymouth, which demonstrates that an understanding of the raw material used in earth construction is essential both for the erection of new buildings and for the conservation of existing, often historically important, earth structures.

COB BUILDING TYPES

The cob building tradition in the south-west is a long one, dating from at least the late fourteenth century up to the late nineteenth century (Fig 8.1). At a conservative estimate, there are thought to be around 50,000 earth structures in Devon alone and Devon contains more

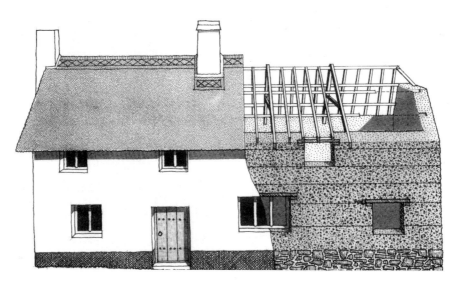

Figure 8.1. A typical seventeenth-century south-western three-room and cross-passage farm house, built of cob with a combed wheat straw roof.

Figure 8.2. Early nineteenth-century cob bank barn at West Forde Farm, Cheriton Fitzpaine, Devon.

Figure 8.3. Brushford Barton, Devon. A substantial early nineteenth-century house.

Figure 8.4. Cob and stone pillars at Sandford, Devon.

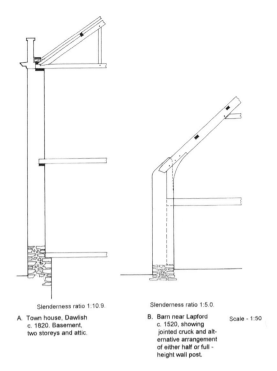

Slenderness ratio 1:10.9.

A. Town house, Dawlish
    c. 1820. Basement,
    two storeys and attic.

Slenderness ratio 1:5.0.

B. Barn near Lapford
    c. 1520, showing
    jointed cruck and alt-
    ernative arrangement
    of either half or full -
    height wall post.

Scale - 1:50

Figure 8.5. Comparison of cob walls, ancient and relatively modern.

surviving late medieval (pre-1540) earth buildings than any other county in Britain (Plate 8.1). The cob buildings of the south-west range in size from the smallest, pig sties and outside privies, up to the largest, threshing barns, cart sheds, chapels, schools, town houses and, in the nine-teenth century, rural and seaside villas (Figs 8.2, 8.3 and 8.4). Some are of great historic interest and therefore enjoy statutory protection. However, the majority re-main unprotected, and the contribution they make to the Devon environment is undervalued.

The earliest cob buildings are known from archaeo-logical excavation and date from at least the thirteenth century. Standing structures exist from the late four-

teenth century and are generally houses of middle status, as stone was preferred for grander buildings. Buildings of the earlier periods tend to have walls of greater thickness (750–800 mm) relative to their height and are roofed with substantial timbers generally of composite cruck types with their feet extending all or part way down into the wall structure (Fig 8.5). These support purlins and secondary rafters under a cladding of wheat thatch or local slate. In the seventeenth and eighteenth centuries these types of roof are replaced by simple A-frames but both these roofs and their predecessors have high collars and pitches of around 45 degrees or less. Although vernacular styles of building are superseded by polite national styles from the mid eighteenth century onwards, cob remained in common use for their construction, although the universal use of lime renders on all but the humblest buildings makes it difficult often to identify whether these are constructed of cob, brick or stone. During the later period from about 1775 and especially in urban areas wall thickness even in 2 or 2.5 storey houses, was reduced to around 600 mm or even less in some cases, and the walls themselves became higher; wall heights up to the eaves of 7 or 8 metres were not uncommon. In the early nineteenth century the use of cob was extended into some categories of public build-ings, such as chapels and schools, and in this later period variations in construction techniques occurred with the composite use of timber and cob (Fig 8.6).

By the 1860s however, with the coming of the railways, improved sea and canal transport, and increasing industrialization, indigenous local materials such as cob and thatch were gradually supplanted by brick, stone, fired clay tiles and slate, particularly in the expanding urban areas (Fig 8.7). The last major cob building to be erected in Devon, before the current cob building re-

Figure 8.6. Sandford School, Devon: apart from the pillars, a wholly cob building of 1825.

vival, was a large house known as Coxen near Budleigh Salterton by the Arts and Crafts designer, Ernest Gimson, completed in 1912.

The plan forms and main constructional details of cob buildings do not show any significant differences from those constructed of masonry, though there are some regional variations. For example, fully hipped and half-hipped roofs, intended to support thatch, are common in Devon whereas in Cornwall, where slate was frequently used, gabled roofs are more common, with the cob taken right up to the apex. Also in Cornwall, lateral or gable end cob chimney stacks often project into the house, unlike the Devon practice, where they are generally built externally, thus providing a buttressing effect to the main walls.

Although the use of cob for building in the south-west, especially in Devon, was ubiquitous for several centuries, it was rarely mentioned in contemporary records. This is primarily a consequence of its common-place nature as a building material in the region, enabling construction with relatively little specialist skill and by techniques handed down through the generations. Moreo-

ver cob was not employed for the grandest buildings (there are no medieval cob churches) and must have been most commonly used at a largely sub-literate level. Salzman quotes a contract of 1478 for a malt house in Exeter to be constructed of 'mudwalle' but this is a rare documentary mention (Salzman 1952). Even in the early nineteenth century, when cob was employed in more formal buildings such as nonconformist chapels, this is not the subject of contemporary comment (Fig 8.8). The agricultural commentators of this period do certainly refer to it and were generally not enthusiastic about it although they appreciated its cheapness. Vancouver in 1808 described it as a 'dull, heavy and deforming material' (Vancouver 1808). With little therefore in the way of documentary references to its use, the study of cob in the south-west has primarily to be archaeology based.

COB CONSTRUCTION METHODS

Cob walls are normally built off a stone plinth, which can vary in height from around 450 mm above ground level up to first floor joist level in some domestic

Figure 8.7. Early nineteenth-century cob urban architecture in Dawlish, south Devon.

Figure 8.8. Early nineteenth-century chapel at Cullompton, Devon. Stripping the render reveals the cob of the walls.

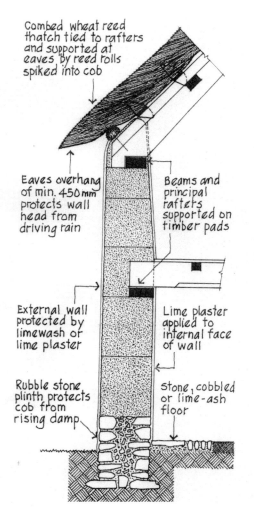

Figure 8.9. Cross-section through a south-western cob wall.

Figure 8.10. Rebuilding a cob extension at Cullacott Werrington, Cornwall in 1995.

buildings (Fig 8.9). Correct mixing of the material is as important as the actual construction process. The soil is first broken down to a fairly fine tilth, all large stones greater than about 50 mm diameter being removed in the process. It is then spread out in a bed some 100 mm in depth on a hard, pre-wetted surface on top of a thin layer of straw. Water is then added and a second, thicker layer of straw is spread evenly on top (about 25 kg of straw per cubic metre of soil, 1.5 to 2.0% by weight, is considered adequate). The straw is then trodden into the soil which is turned several times, more water being added as required. Thorough treading of the mix, traditionally by either men or animals, is vital because it ensures even distribution of the clay and renders the material to a consistency and state of cohesion suitable for building.

In practice much of the necessary compaction was achieved by the workman's boot, the material being placed in diagonal layers, well heeled in, and then thoroughly trodden between each lift (Fig 8.10). The height of a lift or 'raise' would vary according to soil type and consistency from 300 mm up to 900 mm (Plate 8.2). The material always overlapped the face of the stone plinth by at least 75 to 100 mm, the surplus being pared off after a few days, usually before commencing the next lift, with a special flat, sharp-edged spade, known as a 'paring iron', or with a small mattock. The best cob walls

comprise well-graded, moderately clayey soils containing plenty of small stones and straw and have been well compacted. Such walls, if kept dry by means of a stone plinth and a roof with good overhang at the eaves, ideally around 450 mm, will last for centuries.

Occasionally cob was constructed in much smaller lifts of only about 150 mm with the straw being trodden into each lift. During the nineteenth century this method was used in conjunction with simple, moveable shuttering, a system known as 'boxing'. Later in the century the cob was sometimes stabilized with lime, probably in clay-rich soils.

Heights of masonry plinths, as well as the height of individual lifts of cob, show considerable variation throughout the region. Sometimes the most basic, one- or two-room plan cottages had no plinth at all. Cob chimney stacks were commonplace: in nineteenth-century buildings they were often formed within the wall thickness, a common cause of structural problems today. Stone or brick stacks are often later additions to early buildings. Plinth height varied from 300 mm above the ground up to first floor level in some areas, particularly in north Devon, and this was perhaps related to local availability of stone and to its cost (Fig 8.11). Further west in the region cob is used in a more piecemeal fashion mixed often inexplicably with areas of stonework.

THE STATE OF COB IN THE SOUTH-WEST

Although many cob buildings have stood for centuries it has to be accepted that cob represents a 'high maintenance' form of construction. The results of neglect or inappropriate repair and maintenance can have dire consequences, and serious structural failures do occasionally occur. Until recently, there has been a general lack of understanding of the causes of structural failure in cob walls and of the preventative measures needed to avoid their occurrence. Despite the dissemination of advice and guidance on the best means of repairing and maintaining cob buildings, mainly through the publications of the Devon Earth Building Association and the Devon Historic Buildings Trust, there is still much ignorance concerning this issue and examples of bad practice within the building industry abound.

Figure 8.11. Nineteenth-century cob barn at Swimbridge in north Devon. The stone walls of the ground floor are characteristic of this part of Devon.

The number of cob structures lost annually in the region, either through collapse or demolition, is difficult to quantify. In Devon the number is likely to be at least one hundred, probably more if one includes boundary walls. Most of these are likely to be agricultural buildings, whose demise goes unnoticed and therefore unrecorded. Some barns are 'saved', with official sanction, by being converted to residential use. Commonly this means extensive demolition followed by rebuilding in concrete blockwork. Cob buildings are so numerous in some areas that their special interest is undervalued and this leads to a slow attrition of the total stock. It was in response to this situation, and to the worrying problems associated with inappropriate maintenance and inept, uninformed repairs to cob buildings, that the Devon Earth Building Working Group was set up in the spring of 1991. The original group was, as its name suggests, simply a technical, advisory panel with founder members from English Heritage, Teignbridge District Council and the Building Research Establishment.

Having decided that the most effective way to achieve its principal aim was to encourage building industry professionals to adopt a more informed and conservative approach to the repair and maintenance of cob buildings, the group organised a number of seminars. Then, in early 1993, links were established with Plymouth University School of Architecture with a view to setting up joint training and research programmes. This collaboration, which lead to the establishment of the Centre for Earthen Architecture at Plymouth, has proved extremely fruitful. Courses on the conservation of earth buildings as well as new earth construction now form an integral part of the School of Architecture's activities, and a research programme, started in 1993 and dedicated to all aspects of earth construction, is still being actively supported (Fig 8.12). The group has flourished and now forms the steering committee of the Devon Earth Building Association (DEBA) which has over 100 members, with its own newsletter, annual meetings and publications on cob building and repair.

Figure 8.12. Sixteenth-century cob gatehouses at Bury Barton, Lapford, Devon showing the cob repairs carried out in 1994.

Figure 8.13. A large cob house extension being constructed at Black Dog, Devon by Richard Tapp in 1991.

Figure 8.14. Kevin McCabe's new (1993–4) house at Northleigh, east Devon.

The roots of the cob building revival go back to 1980, when Alfred Howard, a master builder from Down St Mary in mid Devon, put up the first entirely new cob building to be erected in Devon since the 1930s (Plate 8.3). During the 1980s, and following the example set by Mr Howard, pioneering cob construction work, albeit on a modest scale, was undertaken by both English Heritage and by the National Trust. However it is mainly during the last 10 years, due principally to the efforts of DEBA and Plymouth School of Architecture, that cob building and major cob repair work has begun to increase really significantly.

For example, at the beginning of the 1990s there were less than a handful of cob builders in Devon, whereas now there are at least 20 with experience of using the material (Fig 8.13). Several new build projects have been successfully completed and various historically important cob structures have undergone major structural repair. Most of the Devon district councils have shown considerable interest in new cob building projects and made significant efforts to help reconcile the demands of the Building Regulations with earth construction. The existence of so very many cob buildings in the south-west has helped in

this regard since it is possible to take the proven viability of these into consideration when assessing proposals for new cob structures for Building Regulation approval under the 1991 Regulations. Two major new cob houses, at Down St Mary and at Northleigh, were constructed with full cooperation from the respective district councils (Fig 8.14). New and more appropriate approaches to the repair of cob using earthen materials and lime-based finishes have also been well supported by them. It is a sign of this sympathetic attitude that Building Control officers sit on the Working Group of DEBA. So, although the underlying problems relating to the conservation of cob buildings still remain, the future holds great promise, and the adoption of raw earth as a material for the construction of low-cost low-energy, 'green' buildings is now a very real possibility.

NOTES

L.F. Salzman, *Building in England down to 1540* (Oxford, 1952), 540.

C. Vancouver, *General View of the Agriculture of Devon* (1808; reprinted New York, August M. Kelley, 1969), 92.

Chapter 9:   Earthen construction in Ireland

Dick Oram

Ireland is blessed with extensive deposits of fine glacial clays, and these have been the basic material for the earthen structures which have been created. The most extensive deposits stretch from Lough Neagh southwards through the midlands to Dublin City and the south-east.

Earthen man-made construction in Ireland can be classified under three broad headings:

FIELD MONUMENTS

The first can be identified as field monuments; they fill a time span of roughly 4000 BC to 1500 AD. Ireland, like Britain, possesses a great wealth and variety of earth monuments.

Surviving structures include grave monuments and burial mounds; ritual and defensive earthworks, ecclesiastical and settlement enclosures and ancient land divisions. Many monument classes can be ascribed to particular periods and many developed as responses to physical, political and social change.

A great number of the earthen monument complexes which survive have very long histories and have been added to and altered over time, leaving a rich and deeply textured patina of remains in the landscape. The work of the two state-sponsored archaeological surveys for the Records of Monuments, North and South, has also given rise to and supported the identification of areas possessing quite widespread, integrated remains of previously unknown monuments, earthworks and associated features.

Some field monuments are particular in character. These range from the almost ubiquitous earthen settlement enclosures, known as ringforts, through to much more impressive hillforts, to the very special royal sites of the Bronze Age and Iron Age such as Rathcroghan, Co.

Westmeath, Eamhain Macha, Co. Armagh, Dun Ailinne, Co. Kildare and Tara, Co. Meath. Their particular range of associated sites include linear earthworks like 'the Dorsey' and sites such as King's Stables within the Navan complex and the linear mounds of Tailteann close to Tara, which remain quite enigmatic in some respects and have deep ritual associations.

Others which have more prosaic and sometimes obvious functions include the very much later medieval linear earthworks around 'the Pale' (the English stronghold around the Dublin region) and the enclosing earthworks around settlements, ecclesiastic sites and early towns, and the much later forts and fortifications of the Tudor period, designed to withstand cannon fire.

All are fragile in today's climate of economic growth, farm development, land use change and significant industrial development.

SIXTEENTH—NINETEENTH CENTURIES

The second group is composed of buildings constructed in the period 1500 to 1900. There is clear evidence of earth buildings existing before 1500 but none of them has survived to the present day. Few earth buildings were built after 1900 and there are few people alive who have witnessed their construction. These buildings were generally dwellings and out-offices intended for either domestic or farm use. They were generally single-storey, but there is a sprinkling of two-storey examples. Earth walls are known in a few three-storey buildings but in such cases, they are not major structural elements. These instances, however, do prove that earth was at one time used extensively at every social level.

Figure 9.1. Hill of Tara, Co. Meath.

Figure 9.2. Dun Ailinne, Co. Kildare.

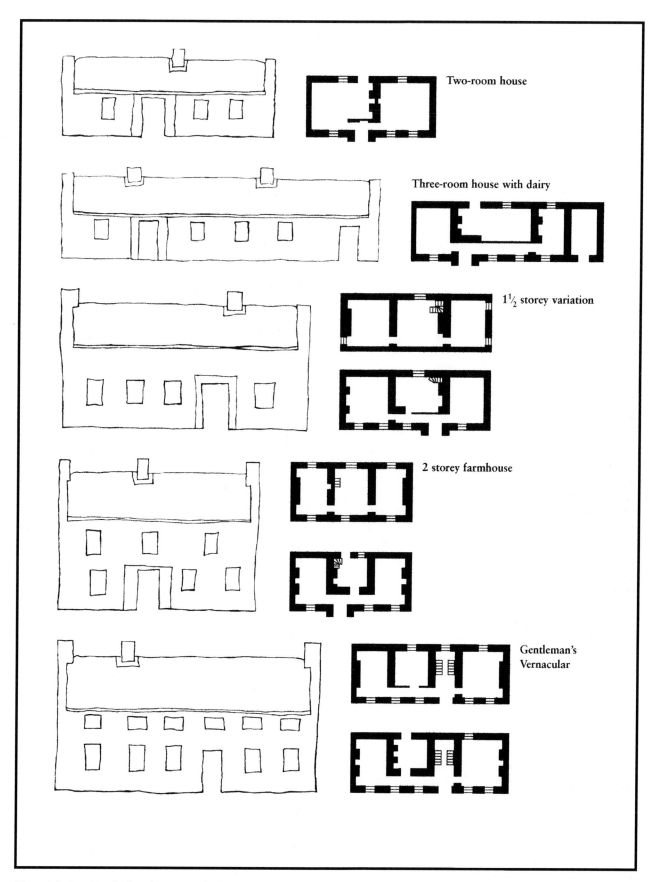

Figure 9.3. Rural mudwall traditions in Ireland.

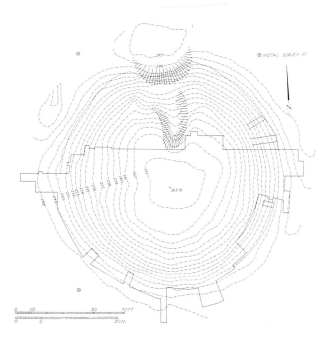

Figure 9.4. Navan fort, Co. Meath. Mound showing limit of excavation.

Figure 9.5. Navan fort, Co. Meath.

A number of different construction techniques can be seen, used side by side or one over the other. The main groupings are:

Mass walling

The clay was either rammed in between shuttering or placed by hand and smarmed into a monolithic mass.

Clay lump

The earth was formed by hand into irregular brick-shaped lumps and dried before being built into the walls using clay slurry for bonding.

Unburned brick

A regular wooden mould was used to form the clay. Sometimes the mould was large enough to make more than one brick at a time. Like the lump, these bricks were dried before use and finally placed in a bed of wet clay as mortar.

Sods

Sods were cut from pasture land, naturally reinforced with roots and other vegetable material. Sometimes a long length was cut, then rolled for transportation to the wall and unrolled in courses, layer on layer. Sometimes it was cut into brick-like chunks. Peat turf

was also used, having been cut into fairly regular shapes using a turfing spade or 'loy'. It is possible that turf was only used for internal partitions.

Reinforced earth construction

The simplest form of reinforced earth construction is straw or other fibrous material beaten into the clay, sometimes in a random fashion but more often in layers or courses. A more sophisticated form of reinforcement is to build in timber members. Cruck framing is one such technique. More or less regular timber box framing with clay infill to the panels is another. In other instances, only horizontal timbers were used, built in as the clay wall was raised. Included in this family of techniques are the wattle and daub walls, where wattle or hurdle is daubed with wet clay from both sides.

Earth was widely used for flooring, even in stone and brick houses, and is commonly found in use as mortar, sometimes alone, or gauged with lime. Frequently, such mortars are reinforced with vegetable and animal fibres and used in conjunction with random rubble masonry.

ENGINEERING AND INDUSTRIAL CONSTRUCTIONS

The third classification is engineering and industrial constructions, generally dating between 1750 and 1900. Examples include canals, mill streams and races, dams, levees, causeway and rampart roads, railway embankments, abutments and cuttings.

Earth buildings in Ireland are generally under-appreciated and not understood by present-day society. Many earth buildings lie in and around the countryside in a ruinous or semi-ruinous state. Sadly, it is very rare to find sympathetic repair and maintenance being undertaken.

Chapter 10: The earth below: 'Earthworks'

BOB BEWLEY AND PAUL EVERSON

DEFINITIONS OF FORM

In England, the most common archaeological usage of the term 'earthwork' is to characterize abandoned archaeological sites that are visible as undulations, as 'humps and bumps', on the land surface, typically in pasture, moorland or waste. It contrasts earthworks on the one hand to standing or ruined buildings and on the other to sites which have been levelled by ploughing or buried by other forms of land use and development. This usage therefore characterizes the current state of survival rather than necessarily the original form or constructional materials of sites. Something of the definition by Hadrian Allcroft nearly a hundred years ago is influential here: for him, earthworks in England:

> include all and any mounds, banks, ditches, walls, pits, etc, whether built of earth or of stone or of both, so long as these show no trace of mortar. It includes such works as the great enclosing banks and fosses of Avebury and Stonehenge, while it excludes the megaliths within them and all similar monuments, menhirs and dolmens, circles of standing stones, stone avenues etc. (Allcroft 1908)

Much more relevantly in a modern context, however, is the circumstance that within the agreed terminology that governs national and local Sites and Monuments Records in England, 'earthworks' is explicitly a descriptor of a current monument form of evidence within a wide range of options (for example, Documentary Evidence or Building, see RCHME 1998). The field remains at Kirkstead Abbey and many castle sites, for example, are for this reason earthworks in English archaeological literature, for all the undoubted fact that in excavation they would produce stone structures of mortared ashlar standing several metres high (Fig 10.1).

Figure 10.1. Kirkstead Abbey, Lincolnshire. TF 1961/18 (National Monuments Record © Crown Copyright).

Figure 10.2. Grainthorpe, Lincolnshire. SE 9501/4 (National Monuments Record © Crown Copyright).

As the appearance of Kirkstead suggests, the detailed form of what are in these terms all 'earthworks' may nevertheless reflect the nature of the original structure and allow, more or less, original details to be perceived without excavation. There is a striking difference in the earthworks of an abandoned nucleated medieval settlement in the stone-rich zones of central England and one in the clay or marshland areas. In the first, house sites are identifiable as grassed foundations and property divisions present as clear banks, for example at Grainthorpe, Lincolnshire (Fig 10.2). In the second, property divisions are ditched, and house sites invisible, as at North Cockerington, Lincolnshire (Plate 10.1). In the latter cases, peasant houses were of earth or earth and wood, 'mud-and-stud', whose form and antiquity has been demonstrated by excavation at Goltho, Lincolnshire (Beresford 1975) and elsewhere. Yet socially, functionally and otherwise these are an identical type of site.

A similar contrast of form but identity of function is found among other medieval sites: manorial complexes that are moated in contrast to stone-walled; castles that were wholly timber and earth (Higham & Barker 1992) in contrast to stone castles (Plate 10.2). The patterns of occurrence clearly relate to geographical and topographical factors, especially to local resources of building materials. Despite cross-cutting social influences, these factors are mirrored in the patterns of local vernacular building patterns across England (Clifton-Taylor 1972).

There is a chronological depth to these contrasts of form but identity of function. Roman military installations survive as earthworks whether their original form was timber and turf (and never upgraded to stone) (Plate 10.3) or stone. A full range of complexity can be found in Hadrian's Wall, one of England's most impressive linear

monuments. Originally this was a turf wall running across the Tyne-Solway gap (some 130 kilometres / 80 miles): its central section was replaced as a stone structure linking numerous forts, fortlets and milecastles, whose earthwork form may also represent an upgrading of turf and timber to stone or stone construction from the start. The same theme may extend back to the fourth millennium BC and the earliest prehistoric enclosures in England, usually referred to as causewayed enclosures. These have predominantly been recorded as earthworks (Plate 10.4) and cropmarks in central southern England but recent research has shown that stone variants in Cornwall, Devon, Cumbria and possibly Northumberland also exist (Oswald et al forthcoming). Indeed, throughout later prehistory the field systems of the Bronze and Iron Ages show interesting similarities of shape and size but are defined by stone boundaries in the uplands and by ditches (visible as cropmarks) in the lowlands.

Visibility

If this usage denoting survival blurs the issue of construction material, it also conceals a sense in which earth and the contrasts between earthen deposits are inherent in the nature of buried sites and our access to them through aerial photography. It is the contrasts in the colourations of the earth revealed in the bare winter soils of arable cultivation that allow the identification, sometimes with startling clarity, of buried sites as soilmarks (Plate 10.5). The effects are localized in England. The need for contrast places a premium on light-toned base soils such as chalk against which ditches filled with humic material can stand out, or dark-toned soils such as peats against which gravel structures or silted features contrast. In an

Plate 10.1. *North Cockerington, Lincolnshire. NMR 12434/27 (National Monuments Record © Crown Copyright).*

Plate 10.2. *Parracombe Motte and Bailey Castle, Exmoor. NMR 15604/21 (National Monuments Record © Crown Copyright).*

Plate 10.3. *Martinhoe Beacon, Exmoor. Small, earthen Roman fortlet NMR 15604/33 (National Monuments Record © Crown Copyright).*

Plate 10.4. *Windmill Hill, Wiltshire. A Neolithic causewayed enclosure. NMR 15403/22 (National Monuments Record © Crown Copyright).*

Plate 10.5. Soilmarks of Neolithic enclosures, south of Rudston, East Yorkshire. NMR12216/34 (National Monuments Record © Crown Copyright).

Plate 10.6. Round barrows at Witchampton, Dorset; the mounds in the process of degradation, revealed as cropmarks in a field of peas. SU 0006/11 (National Monuments Record © Crown Copyright).

Plate 10.8. Wan's Dyke, Wiltshire. NMR 15583/24 (National Monuments Record © Crown Copyright).

Plate 10.7. Yarnbury hillfort, Wiltshire. The longevity of use at this site is revealed by an inner, neolithic, enclosure, then the outer, later prehistoric, hillfort; finally the rectangular features are the remnants of a medieval market. NMR 15406/18 (National Monuments Record © Crown Copyright).

Plate 10.9. Avebury, stone circle and henge, with Silbury Hill in the distance. NMR 15419/06 (National Monuments Record © Crown Copyright).

Plate 10.10. Strip lynchets in Wiltshire. NMR 15207/14 (National Monuments Record © Crown Copyright).

Plate 10.11. Circular prehistoric monuments visible as cropmarks beneath a small area of ridge and furrow near Peterborough, Cambridgeshire. NMR 15381/1 (National Monuments Record © Crown Copyright).

Plate 10.12. Rabbit warrens at Douthwaite Dale, North Yorkshire. NMR 12062/8 (National Monuments Record © Crown Copyright).

Plate 10.13. Chipping Camden, Gloucestershire. Formal garden of c 1610. NMR 3152/17 (National Monuments Record © Crown Copyright).

analogous way, it is the contrast in the moisture-retaining potential of different earthen deposits, natural subsoil against filled man-made features, when exacerbated by conditions of soil moisture deficiency, that produces effects in growing crops, producing cropmarks recorded by aerial photography (Wilson 1982; Riley 1987).

Context: position and symbolism

All this said, England is remarkably rich in earthworks which combine above-ground visibility with earthen structures resulting from deliberate use of the material for construction. They comprise a formally, functionally and chronologically diverse body of the archaeological resource, which there is space here to treat only selectively and by example. Furthermore, much of this resource is not discrete and detached as archaeological items (though that is the form in which it is most easily illustrated); rather it is embedded within the modern landscape, contributing to its diversity and locally distinctive historic character (Fairclough 1999).

Many of the earliest field monuments had ritual and symbolic purposes and deployed massed earthen structures in conjunction with careful siting within the landscape to achieve visibility. Their parent material, most obviously in the case of chalk, will have given them a striking appearance when new. Perhaps the best example of this are the thousands of round barrows in southern England on the chalk downland (Plate 10.6). These barrows are clearly built from the earth; the mound material being provided from the circular surrounding ditch; this fresh mound would stand out as a white beacon for some considerable time after the initial burial and the frequent reuse and secondary burials attest to the important positions these sites occupy in the landscape.

Major hillforts, too, exhibit attributes of large earth-moving in their construction, as well as occupying prominent positions in the landscape. They, too, must have been made more visible by exposing the bedrock (especially chalk) to view (Plate 10.7).

Large linear boundaries have also carved out large swathes of earth, leaving prominent ditches and banks. Striking examples are the Wansdyke in Wessex, a boundary whose origins are thought to lie in the prehistoric period (Plate 10.8) or Offa's Dyke, dating from the eighth century AD, that runs the length of the border between Wales and England.

The particular importance of selected places is reflected in their repeated and accumulative marking by successive monuments of different forms, whether by the addition or extension of earthen monuments as at Yarnbury or Whitesheet Hill, Wilts, or through a mixture of earthen and stone remains, as at Avebury or Stonehenge. Such well-marked foci are now commonly perceived as having been the centre-pieces or major components of extensive ritual landscapes, whose limits may be both positively defined by the concentration of monuments, together with natural landforms and cultural linkages, and negatively by surrounding contemporary land-use (Plate 10.9).

Agriculture

In addition to the individual settlements, ritual or defensive sites, there is a whole range of earthworks in England which are the result of a variety of cultivation techniques and exploitation of the soil for farming. These are the residual, deliberate or consequential results of agriculture; fields are in several senses earth constructions. The earliest forms are the prehistoric field systems which can be seen in the landscape today in a number of places but especially at West Penwith in Cornwall and on the reave systems on Dartmoor (Fleming 1988). Here, the earth construction is effectively the cultivable land created by clearance of a stony surface or by boundary creation. Elsewhere in England, many field systems are visible only through cropmarks and soilmarks as so much of the prime agricultural land has been intensively ploughed since 1945 (Palmer 1984; Stoertz 1997). However, there are remarkable islands of survival of early field systems, the so-called Celtic fields (Bowen 1961), most notably on Salisbury Plain. The deliberate formation of strip lynchets on the steep-sided chalkland slopes of central England is an indication of the importance of maximizing output on good soils. Their substantial construction and their location has commonly meant they are less vulnerable to subsequent destruction (Plate 10.10).

In the medieval period the development of vast landscapes of open, common townfield systems (Hall 1995) throughout the Central Settlement Province of midland England (Roberts & Wrathmell forthcoming) has left a legacy in ridge-and-furrow cultivation remains, ridges of earth separated by furrows, that has been perhaps the most extensive earthen monument in Britain, if not Europe. Even the prevalence of ridge-and-furrow as an earthwork field monument in England has severely diminished in the face of the mechanization and intensification of agriculture, especially arable cultivation, over the past fifty years. What through its commonplace survival was until recently a monument type thought inappropriate for formal protection is now being assessed as a priority to identify a sustainable, effective conservation prescription. Ridge-and-furrow has even been shown in some circumstances to have preserved earlier monuments, the best example being at Maxey, near Peterborough (Plate 10.11). By contrast, the removal of ridge-and-furrow on the chalk Wolds of Eastern Yorkshire by intensive modern arable (Stoertz 1997) has also led to the erosion of the earlier Neolithic and Bronze Age monuments beneath (see Plate 10.5).

Other distinctive forms of agricultural regime based on earthen monuments relate to water management, both delivering it for productive improvement and removing or excluding it. They include the water meadows of the river valleys of the Wessex chalkland, mostly of the seventeenth to nineteenth centuries. Land reclamation schemes of medieval and early modern date, familiar on the coast of eastern England, mirror those along the continental North Sea littoral (Cook & Williamson 1999).

In recent centuries, the identifiable diversity of *earthen* earthworks has increased in both large and small ways. A very specialized form of farming, that of rabbit warrening, has contributed groups of earthen mounds to the English archaeological landscape. Known as 'pillow mounds', they can be confused with earlier burial monuments. Though some date from the medieval period, those found in clusters of square or linear arrangements, often on marginal agricultural land, were the factories for rabbit fur and meat of the post-medieval and early modern era (Plate 10.12).

In the sixteenth, seventeenth and early eighteenth centuries, massed earthen structures in the form of terraces, raised walks and mounts, characteristically arranged as components in geometrical layouts, underpinned the formal gardens that routinely accompanied the houses of the nobility and gentry of the age (Plate 10.13). Their occurrence was a social and cultural phenomenon, transcending regional patterns of building materials. Surprisingly large numbers survive as archaeological remains, whether abandoned or embedded in later layouts. The scale and stability of construction recalls the skills inherent in military deployment of earthen defence works. Even the advent of the naturalistic fashion of landscaped parks brought with it movement of earth on a large scale to create views and effects, for example with lakes and dams and graded sloping lawns that form the archaeological components of such landscapes (Plate 10.13).

Industry

In apparent contrast, former industrial complexes, so often exemplified by their stone, brick or metal superstructures, are commonly marked as archaeological remains by massive earthen deposits either as dumps, tippings or mounds. Usually these are waste deposits or residue, but they still required constructing. In the same way many of the railway embankments or canal constructions required a high degree of engineering skill, using either primary earth, the soil in surrounding fields or the spoil from an adjacent cutting, or the use of waste deposits from nearby industrial processes. The blast banks or 'traverses' surrounding danger building at factory sites handling explosives production, notably at the Royal Gunpowder Factory at Waltham Abbey, represent a deliberate exploitation of special qualities of earth, for this purpose superior to metal, brick or concrete (Cocroft forthcoming).

This paper has skimmed over the incidence and significance of earth and earthwork construction in England over six thousand years and has highlighted some examples that contribute to this country's rich archaeological legacy. It is perhaps worth concluding with the thought that the defence of these islands has often been built of earth whether through fortifications made of earth and stone, as are well preserved at Tilbury, Portsmouth or Berwick, or through the construction of airfields in the 1940s, so many of which were and still remain no more than smoothed grassy fields.

NOTES

A. H. Allcroft, *Earthwork of England* (London: 1908).

F. Beresford, *The Medieval Village: Excavations at Goltho and Barton Blount,* Society for Medieval Archaeology Monograph Series 6 (London: Society for Medieval Archaeology, 1975).

C. Bowen, *Ancient Fields,* (London: British Association for the Advancement of Science, 1961).

A. Clifton-Taylor, *The Pattern of English Building* (London: 1972).

W. D. Cocroft, *Dangerous Energy. The Archaeology of Gunpowder and Military Explosives Manufacture,* (London: English Heritage, forthcoming).

Cook and Williamson, *Water Management in the English Landscape. Field, Marsh and Meadow* (Edinburgh: 1999).

G. Fairclough, *Historic Landscape Characterisation,* (London: English Heritage, 1999).

A. Fleming, *The Dartmoor Reaves* (London: Batsford, 1988).

D. Hall, *The Open Fields of Northamptonshire,* (Northampton: Northampton Record Society, 1995).

R. Higham, and P. Barker, *Timber Castles* (London: Batsford, 1992).

A. Oswald, M. Barber and C. Dyer *Neolithic Causewayed Enclosures,* (London: English Heritage, forthcoming).

R. Palmer, *Danebury An Iron Age Hillfort in Hampshire, An Aerial Photographic Interpretation of its Environs.* RCHME Supplementary Series No. 6 (Swindon: RCHME, 1984).

D. N. Riley, *Air Photography and Archaeology,* (London: Duckworth, 1987).

B. K. Roberts and S. Wrathmell, *An Atlas of Rural Settlement in England,* (London: English Heritage, forthcoming).

C. Stoertz, *Ancient Landscapes of the Yorkshire Wolds: Aerial Photographic Transcription and Analysis.* (Swindon: RCHME, 1997).

D. R. Wilson, *Air Photo Interpretation for Archaeologists* (London: Batsford, 1982).

ACKNOWLEDGEMENTS

The staff of the National Monuments Record in the Enquiry Research Team and the darkrooms have been immensely helpful in providing the information, permissions and images at short notice and we are very grateful. We also thank Val Johnson for her skill in reading two hand-written manuscripts and combining them into a single typed text.

Chapter 11:   Unbaked earth and world heritage

PHILIP WHITBOURN OBE

It was back in the third quarter of the twentieth century, in the year 1972 to be precise, that the General Conference of the United Nations Educational, Scientific and Cultural Organization (UNESCO) adopted the 'Convention concerning the protection of the world cultural and natural heritage', popularly known as the 'World Heritage Convention'. Among other provisions the Convention, which is managed by the World Heritage Committee, assisted by the World Heritage Centre in UNESCO Secretariat and advised by ICOMOS and the IUCN, provides for the identification of a World Heritage List of cultural and natural properties of 'outstanding universal value to humankind as a whole'.

When the year 2000 was reached, UNESCO had inscribed 480 Cultural World Heritage Sites, together with 128 Natural Sites and 22 Mixed Sites. These are distributed around 118 countries, in all five continents. That works out at an average of little more than five Sites per country, so the list is a highly selective one, as indeed it should be if it is really to represent world heritage of outstanding value to all humankind.

Not surprisingly, stone is a material that features prominently in many of the Cultural World Heritage Sites, such as the great pyramids and rock tombs of ancient Egypt, and the masterpieces of classical Greek art on the Acropolis at Athens. Brick features as a building material on many of the Sites too, as in the historic Mosque City of Bagerhat in Bangladesh. So does wood, as at Bryggen, the old wharf of Bergen in Norway, for instance. Unbaked earth also takes its place in the palette of materials that make up the picture of the planet's cultural heritage, as seen through the eyes of UNESCO's World Heritage Committee. The Ksar of Ait-Ben-Haddou, a group of earthen buildings in

Southern Morocco, is one example, and the traditional Ashanti buildings northeast of Kumasi in Ghana is another, while a third is the unbaked brick archaeological site in the Indus Valley at Moenjodaro, Pakistan, dating from the Third Millennium BC.

In the UK, unbaked earth forms a significant element of several of the country's Cultural World Heritage Sites. At Avebury in Wiltshire, the massive bank and ditch of the henge stand out as monumentally vast, and enclose an area of some 11.5 ha (28.5 acres) (Fig 11.1). The bank is about 1.3 km (four-fifths of a mile) in length, and now stands some 5 m (14–18 ft) above ground level. Originally it stood 16.7 m (55 ft) above a 9 m (30 ft) deep square-bottomed ditch, although about half of the depth of the latter has become silted up over the course of the last four and a half thousand years or so. No less spectacular is the enigmatic Neolithic Silbury Hill at Avebury (Fig 11.2). This is the largest man-made mound in Europe, comparable in size and age with some of the smaller pyramids at Giza. The base of the mound is almost circular and covers an area of 2.2 ha (5.25 acres). The hill is 40 m (130 ft) high and contains about 350,000 m³ (12,500 cu ft) of chalk and soil. The first of its three phases of construction consisted of turves, still full of ants, some of whose remains survived. The turves were stacked up in a staked-out area, and covered with consecutive layers of soil, clay, chalk and gravel. On top of this, two further phases of soil and chalk-block construction gave the mound its present conical shape. Other major earthen features of the Stonehenge/Avebury World Heritage Site include West Kennet Long Barrow at Avebury, dating from around 3700 BC and, at Stonehenge, the Cursus and Bronze Age barrow groups.

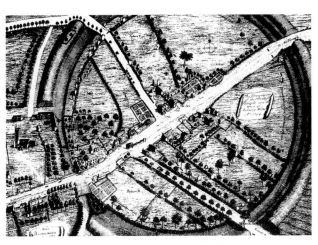

Figure 11.1. William Stukeley's eighteenth-century plan of the Great Henge at Avebury.

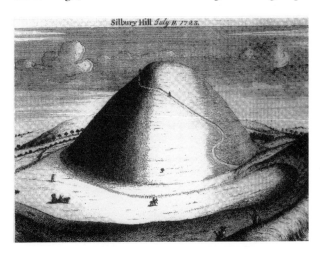

Figure 11.2. William Stukeley's sketch of Silbury Hill in 1723.

Figure 11.3. Erosion at Avebury.

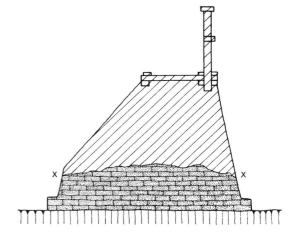

Turf Wall

Built in coursed turves: 45 x 30 x 15 cm

Figure 11.4. Cross-section showing the probable original form of the turf wall at the Cumbrian end of Hadrian's Wall.

Erosion is a matter that has to be addressed within the Stonehenge/Avebury World Heritage Site (Fig 11.3). At Silbury Hill, fencing has been used in an attempt to keep people off the slopes. This, however, has not proved entirely effective and has had the effect of detracting from the close views of the mound from its base. Thus a major issue has been that of trying to strike a balance between controlling access on the one hand, and minimizing the intrusion of unsightly fencing on the other.

At Maes Howe, in the Neolithic Orkney World Heritage Site, off the northern coast of the Scottish mainland, the chamber tomb, one of the finest in Europe, has stone around the chambers themselves, as has the Kennet Long Barrow. However, whereas the earth mound at West Kennet is long and narrow, around 100 m (300 ft) in length and around 20 m (65 ft) in width, the mound at Maes Howe is a conical-shaped hill, with a diameter of about 28 m (92 ft) and a height of some 11 m (36 ft).

Moving to the Roman era, one may not immediately think of unbaked earth as a material that would be much favoured. Yet it should be remembered that the whole of the western 48 km (30 miles) of Hadrian's Wall was originally built of turf (Fig 11.4). Turf could be cut locally with comparative ease and stacked to form a substantial barrier in a relatively short space of time. When the major Roman fort at Birdoswald, in the Cumbrian part of the Hadrian's Wall World Heritage Site was constructed, a section of the turf wall had to be removed to accommodate the new stone-built fort, which originally lay astride the turf wall. Later, however, when the turf wall was rebuilt in stone, the wall line was moved northwards, so that it met the northern corners of the fort. Although not a great deal of evidence of the turf wall can now be seen, it remains important in the

archaeology of the World Heritage Site. It seems probable that the turf wall was about 3.6 m (12 ft) high, taking account of the 6 m (20 ft) width of the prepared base, and the likely angle at which turves could be laid to form a substantial barrier. The cut blocks of turf were laid in courses and measured about 45 x 30 x 15 cm (1'6" x 1'0" x 6"). A section through the turf wall showed its striped or laminated structure, in alternate blocks of whitish bleached humus and streaks of carbonized grass.

The World Heritage Site at Durham is, as the poet and novelist Sir Walter Scott so aptly described the grey towers, 'Half church of God, half castle 'gainst the Scot'. The 'hill-island' peninsular at Durham is ideal for a fortress, protected as it is on three sides by the steep gorge of the River Wear. Just the neck at the north of the peninsular presented a vulnerable point and it was here

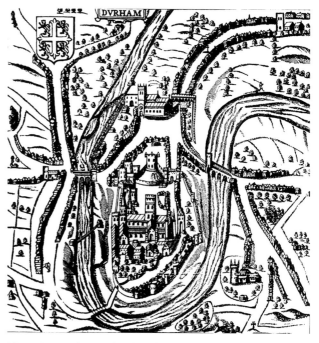

Figure 11.5. John Speed's plan of Durham in 1611, showing the conical earthen 'motte' overlooking the North Gate to the peninsula.

that the Normans laid out the Castle on their typical 'motte-and-bailey' plan. The 'motte' in such castles consisted of a conical mound, and the 'bailey' referred to the courtyard at the foot of the motte. The motte at Durham was positioned to overlook the main entry to the peninsular, which was through the north gate (Fig 11.5). Originally, the motte was probably surmounted by a timber tower. As the Norman fortress became, in turn, a medieval castle, then a palace of the Prince Bishop of Durham, and finally a college of Durham University, the motte was terraced and raised.

Within the Canterbury World Heritage Site there are two earthen campanile mounds. One of these, at St Augustine's Abbey, was probably surmounted by a fifteenth-century timber bell tower, and the mound still affords fine views over the Site. At the Cathedral the detached bell tower, known as the Clocarium, was on a raised mound adjoining what is now the new education centre. Canterbury also has survivals of unbaked earth within standing buildings, especially those of timber-framed construction.

Thus, be it in prehistoric, Roman, Norman or later examples, unbaked earth in the British Isles clearly occupies a significant place in the range of materials forming part of the world's heritage, as identified by the World Heritage Committee of UNESCO.

Chapter 12: The past informing the future: British earth building in the new Millennium

LINDA WATSON

Knowledge of current building practice across the world is readily available through travel, the Internet and published literature. A global survey shows many countries to be using raw earth in the construction of new buildings; either continuing traditional forms, or pursuing a much more contemporary architectural language. In some countries the earth building tradition has never been broken, earth continually providing a readily available and appropriate building material. Other countries, which have lost that tradition, are reconsidering the positive inherent characteristics of earth as a construction material and reintroducing it for current building. Countries such as Australia consider earth a high-status material (Fig 12.1) and the most architecturally fashionable buildings boast unrendered, load-bearing earth walls, whilst Germany for instance is interested in the solutions earth provides to the question of producing sustainable, 'ecologically friendly' architecture. Globally, tradition, fashion and sustainability, together with economy, are some of the reasons earth is being selected for buildings today.

There are signs that an earth renaissance is beginning in Britain but it is yet to make any significant impact on our contemporary building stock. Only a handful of pioneers had achieved new earth building by the end of the twentieth century. Their contribution has created very significant foundations for this renaissance to take hold in the new century, providing important precedents for those who are to follow in achieving successful solutions.

It is curious that the legacy left by past generations of British earth builders has not inspired recent architecture, although it provides a valuable, useable living heritage (Fig 12.2). This is particularly curious when the British interest in heritage is taken in to consideration: why has this not influenced new earth buildings to sympathize with existing settlements? Nor has our growing concern for environmental issues and the pursuit of sustainable architecture generated much activity in earth building. This is probably a consequence of the lack of public and professional awareness in Britain. TERRA

Figure 12.1. A suburban dwelling from Perth, Western Australia showing the rammed earth technique. (Linda Watson)

Figure 12.2. Cob Cones for Chagford Arts Festival 1999 by Jill Smallcombe and Jackie Abey. (Jill Smallcombe)

Figure 12.3. Cottage at Lower Tribcombe, near Honiton, East Devon (1993/94) built by Kevin McCabe using the traditional cob technique. (Linda Watson)

a.

b.

Figure 12.4. Reception Building near Corfe Castle Dorset (1998-1999) designed by Robert Nother, Purbeck District Council, using the traditional cob technique: (a) details of window in north-west elevation; (b) perspective from north-west. (Robert Nother)

2000, the eighth international conference on the study and conservation of earthen architecture, the British Earth Building Exhibition, this and other publications could rectify the situation at the dawn of this new millennium. Public awareness is essential to create the demand for new buildings made from earth, and acceptance that those that are being constructed are being built from a durable and sustainable material. Likewise, professionals must develop an awareness of and familiarity with the material to enable appropriate design, specification, supervision, construction and maintenance of earthen architecture. Earth will probably be restricted to the construction of walls in buildings and landscapes in this country, although its traditional use as flooring material and a surface finish may be revisited for contemporary building.

Architects will admit that the design of a building is a complex process with a wide range of parameters determining the final solution. A significant factor is the choice of the walling material, which makes a considerable contribution to the quality of the architecture. In building with earth, the point in the design process at which the decision to use earth is taken is critical, especially if the designer is unfamiliar with the characteristics of the material. Ideally, the decision should be taken at the outset and the designer should develop the scheme as information accumulates through the architect's own endeavours or through collaboration with consultants.

The first, fundamental question is to determine whether suitable material exists on site, whether any deficiency can be rectified by additives or an alternative source can be located. Enquiries received by the Centre of Earthen Architecture (CEA) at the University of Plymouth are generated mainly through interest in the utilization of on-site materials. Where the proposed site is surrounded by existing earth buildings there are likely to be suitable materials. This is not always the case, sometimes because much of the earthen heritage has been lost.

CEA is a multidisciplinary group of academics working in collaboration with the Devon Earth Building Association (DEBA). Test procedures have been established by CEA, based on established and internationally-agreed techniques, to take samples from sites and laboratory-test those samples. CEA research programmes and continuing collaboration with organizations such as ENTPE (École

National Travaux Public État), Lyon, France, support CEA in the interpretation of test results and advise on suitability and the need for modification.

Disappointment for CEA came from consultancy for the Earth Centre at Doncaster. Both the name and the ethos of the buildings and the site suggested earth would be an appropriate walling material. However, on-site material was unsuitable and bringing other material from which the walls could be constructed from further afield would bring into question the sustainable nature of earth when transportation is taken into consideration. This, together with a number of other problems meant that earth was dismissed as unsuitable (Harries and Clark

Figure 12.5. Building of rammed earth wall of the Visitors' Centre Eden Project, St Austell, Cornwall, designed by Nicholas Grimshaw Partners and constructed by In Situ Rammed Earth Company. (Linda Watson)

Figure 12.6. West Lake Brake, Heybrook Bay Plymouth, (1997-1998), designed by David Sheppard and constructed by the Cob Construction Company. (Linda Watson)

1996). Even so, this consultancy did demonstrate the important contribution of laboratory testing on design decisions.

Recent research at CEA has shown that, traditionally, suitable earth may have been taken from a pit, in a similar way to the quarrying of building stone, to supply the builders of the village (Ford 1998). Transportation did not appear to be an issue, although the earth was dragged a short distance from the periphery of the settlement. While there is no reason why this practice cannot be continued, excessive transportation, with its associated environmental pollution and cost, would deny the inherent sustainable characteristic of earth. Generally, where on-site materials are appropriate, landscaping, engineering or building excavation on the site provides sufficient surplus material for building purposes – as Kevin McCabe demonstrated at his earth building complex, Lower Tricombe, near Honiton, East Devon (1993-94). In addition, the use of on-site earth avoids the large-scale, centralized extraction of alternative walling materials, which contributes to landscape degradation and ecological imbalance (Houben 1995, 5).

Once the suitability of materials is established, the techniques with which the earth can be utilized in the construction of walls must be determined. The nature of the site material may well indicate the appropriate technique, likewise the architectural language of the final solution. The latter may be generated by the need to sympathize with the existing building of the area or maintain regional identity. This implies a continuation of the traditional technique to achieve a traditional form (Fig 12.3) or a contemporary form (Fig 12.4). It may be that the continued use of the material but a different technique would achieve a sympathetic result. Alternatively, the architectural language may not be derived from contextual principles, and other constructional techniques could be considered appropriate; for instance, to achieve a more 'high-tech' solution utilizing the smooth, machine-like visual characteristics of rammed earth with steel and glass. This aesthetic is popular in Western Australia (Fig 12.1). Rammed earth is the technique used to achieve a major wall at the visitors' centre of the Eden Project, St Austell, Cornwall by In Situ Rammed Earth Company (Fig 12.5). The same

technique created the walls of West Lake Brake (Fig 12.6). The diversity of architectural languages possible with the use of earth is an important characteristic of the material.

The range of techniques possible using earth is vast, particularly if the combination of earth with other materials is taken into consideration (Gillaud and Houben 1994). Each technique has its own manufacturing design consideration but it must be recognized that constructional issues require the skills within the local construction industry to achieve the required result. The client may be prepared to pay extra to use a national or even an international labour force, which can be beneficial if the 'imported' labour teaches the local builders. The decisions concerning techniques are very complex and may be generated by a strong belief in using local labour and traditional practice. Specialist contractors have been established in this country to practice the rammed earth technique, including In Situ Rammed Earth, London, and Earth Structures (Europe) Ltd, Market Harborough.

The preparation of the material and the manufacture of the building components utilizing most techniques, require 'low technology' and little energy. Architect Gernot Minke, researching at University of Kassel, Germany, has tabulated the amount of energy required in the manufacture of building products and shown earth to require only 1% of the energy required to manufacture burnt brick or concrete elements. (Minke 1994, 70). The recyclable characteristic of the material caused by the reaction earth undergoes when transformed into a building product is reversible, which means there is no industrial waste and machinery is easily cleaned. (Wimmel 1995). This is very important today with our problems of waste disposable and the relatively high percentage of overall waste which can be attributed to the building industry. Neither does the earth building process produce any toxic chemicals or gases assisting in the buildup of acid rain, ozone depletion and other environmental catastrophes (Houben 1995, 6).

Financial investment in manufacturing equipment is low and this, together with the simplicity of the production process, makes the material very accessible (Houben 1995, 6). There is no mystery involved, as delightfully described by Alfred Howard, who equates building with

Figure 12.7. Ken and Carole Neal's cob home under construction, Newbury, Berkshire, 1999. (Ken Neal)

cob in Devon with the swallows building their nests. Both use the same materials – earth and straw. Mr Howard also advises that the optimum time to build cob is when the swallows are in Britain, as the weather is favourable.

Low technology, together with the availability of free on-site materials makes cob an ideal material for those wishing to construct their own dwellings. In Berkshire, Ken and Carole Neal are using cob techniques to build their own home (Fig 12.7), helped by a mortgage from the Ecology Building Society (Anon. 1999/2000). Maharishi School Sports and Arts Centre, a self building community, is also currently on site in Skelmersdale. Here, rammed earth is being used under the guidance of Roland Keable. Becky Little has built a cob outbuilding at Pitlochry in Scotland, and planning permission has been obtained for mud-and-stud buildings in Lincolnshire and a pisé structure in Norfolk.

Although earth has been used traditionally in British buildings, inspectors, insurers and designers expect to know how earth walls perform numerically. Average values are available, but the variation in raw material, manufacturing and construction techniques means these figures can never be absolute. *Cob and the Building Regulations*, published by DEBA, is particularly supportive for those considering cob in a new building (Devon Earth Building Association 1996).

There is much to still be learnt in Britain about the performance of earth, particularly where the application is in a non-standard design situation, uses a non-traditional construction technique or derives from an unusual subsoil or additive. In cases such as these, our existing earthen heritage can provide little comfort in knowing whether to expect a successful solution.

Many inhabitants of earth buildings claim 'the feelgood factor' to be one of its greatest assets. Gernot Minke believes this to be related to the constant relative humidity of 50% within earth buildings. This is the optimum level for a healthy respiratory system;

over eight years, measurement of Minke's own house were shown to vary by only 5% throughout the year (Minke 1994, 73). Others claim there is great satisfaction to be gained from the occupation of a building erected from natural material taken from beneath the ground upon which your home rests. And rests is just what it does: when there is no longer any need for the building, the earth walls will return to the ground from which they came and the cycle is complete. The reaction, which causes subsoil to change into a suitable building material, is reversible, creating no redundant material to be disposed of. What better credentials for a sustainable building material? Earth is likely to have considerable impact upon the British buildings of this new millennium.

NOTES

Anon, Highs and lows of green building! in *The Ecology Building Society Newsletter*, **18**, (Winter 1999/2000).

Devon Earth Building Association (DEBA), Cob and the Building Regulations, (Devon, DEBA, 1996).

Ford M., *The Development of a Methodology for Creating an Earthen Building Inventory*. Unpublished thesis in preparation at Centre for Earthen Architecture, University of Plymouth, (1998).

Harries W. J. R. and Clark D., *An Investigation of 'Aggregate Claystone' Mix from Cadeby Quarry, Doncaster*, Unpublished consultancy report prepared by Centre for Earthen Architecture, University of Plymouth, (1996).

Guillaud H. and Houben H., *Earth Construction*, Intermediate Technology Publications, **5** (London 1994).

Houben H., Earthen Architecture and Modernity, in *Out of Earth II*, Watson L. and Harries W.J.R. (eds), conference proceedings, University of Plymouth (Plymouth 1995).

Minke G., The Building Material Earth: its properties and possibilities to refine them, in *Out of Earth*, Watson L. and Harding S. (eds) conference proceedings, University of Plymouth (Plymouth 1994).

Wimmel B., *Prima Materia – the earth building material rediscovered*, video by Nord Film Produktionsgemeinschaft (1995).

Further reading

PETER TROTMAN

Ashurst J and Ashurst N,1988 *Brick, Terracotta and Earth*, English Heritage Technical Handbook **2**: Practical Building Conservation:, Aldershot, Gower Press.

Brunskill R W, 1972 *A Handbook of Vernacular Architecture*, London, Faber and Faber.

Department of Scientific and Industrial Research, 1922 *Building in Cob and Pisé de Terre*, Building Research Special Report No 5, London, HMSO.

Devon Earth Building Association, 1993 *Appropriate Plasters, Renders and Finishes for Cob and Random Stone Walls*, Exeter, Devon Earth Building Association.

Devon Historic Buildings Trust, 1988 *Looking After the Outside of Your House*, Devon, Devon Historic Buildings Trust.

Devon Historic Buildings Trust, 1992 *The Cob Buildings of Devon, 1. History, Building Methods and Conservation*, Exeter, Devon Historic Buildings Trust.

Egeland P, 1988 *Cob and Thatch*, Devon, Devon Books.

Harrison R, 1999 *Earth, the Conservation and Repair of Bowhill, Exeter: Working with Cob*, English Heritage Research Transactions, **3**, London, English Heritage.

Houben H and Guillaud H, 1994 *Earth Construction; A Comprehensive Guide*, London, Intermediate Technology Publications.

ICCROM, 1993 *Bibliography on the Preservation, Restoration and Rehabilitation of Earthen Architecture*, Rome, CRATerre/EAG/ICCROM.

Keefe L, 1993 *The Cob Buildings of Devon, 2. Repair and Maintenance*, Exeter, Devon Historic Buildings Trust.

Ley T and Widgery M, 1996 *Cob and the Building Regulations*, Exeter, Devon Earth Building Association.

McCann J, 1983 (1995) *Clay and Cob Buildings*, (2nd edn), Princes Risborough, Shire.

Martin A, 1986 Witchert buildings of Buckinghamshire, in *Country Life*, 2 October.

Norton J, 1986 *Building with Earth. A Handbook*, Intermediate Technology Development Group, Rugby, IT Publications.

Oliver, P, 1999 *Encyclopaedia of Vernacular Architecture*, Oxford, Oxford University Press.

Pearson G T, 1992 *Conservation of Clay and Chalk Buildings*, London, Donhead.

Vale B, 1973 *A Review of the Ministry of Agriculture's Earth Houses*, University of Cambridge, Department of Architecture, Autonomous Housing Study Working Paper 17, Cambridge.

Walker B, McGregor C, Little R, 1996 *Earth Structures and Construction in Scotland,* Historic Scotland Technical Advice Note 6, Edinburgh, Historic Scotland.

Warren, J,1999 *Conservation of Earth Structures*, Oxford, Butterworth-Heinemann.

Watson L, Harries R, 1995 *Out of Earth II*, National Conference on Earth Buildings, Plymouth School of Architecture, Plymouth.

Watson L (ed), 1994-5 Out of Earth 1994 *Proceedings 1ˢᵗ UK International Conference on Earth Buildings, Centre for Earthen Architecture, University of Plymouth*, Plymouth, University of Plymouth.

Williams-Ellis C, Eastwick-Field J, Eastwick-Field E, 1947 *Building in Cob, Pisé and Stabilized Earth*, London, Country Life Ltd.

Williams-Ellis C,1919 *Cottage Building in Cob, Pisé, Chalk and Clay*, London, Newnes and Country Life.

Wright A, 1990 *Craft techniques for Traditional Buildings*, London, Batsford.

6ᵗʰ International Conference on the Conservation of Earthen Architecture, 1990 *Adobe 90 Preprints*, Santa Monica, Getty Conservation Institute.

Bibliography

Regional authors were asked to supply a bibliography specific to the region described. The conventions used vary, and the editors view this list as a useful signpost rather than a definitive bibliography.

WALES

Davies M, 1991 *Save the Last of the Magic: Traditional Qualities of the West Wales Cottage*, Llandysul.

Lowe J B, 1985 *Welsh Country Workers' Housing* 1775–1875, Cardiff, National Museum of Wales.

Nash G D, 1995 *Timber-framed Buildings in Wales*, Cardiff, National Museum of Wales.

Smith P, 1988 *Houses of the Welsh Countryside*, 2nd ed, HMSO.

William E, 1982 Peasant architecture in Caernarvonshire, in *Transactions of the Caernarvonshire Historical Society*, **43**, 83–107.

William E, 1988 *Home-made Homes: Dwellings of the Rural Poor in Wales*, Cardiff, National Museum of Wales.

THE SOLWAY PLAIN

Brunskill RW, 1962 The clay houses of Cumberland, in *Transactions of the Ancient Monuments Society*, **10**.

Brunskill R W, 1974 *Vernacular Architecture of the Lake Counties*, London, Faber and Faber.

Dickinson W, 1852 The Farming of Cumberland, in *The Journal of the Royal Agricultural Society of England*, **13** (pt II), London.

Dickinson W, 1859 *A Glossary of Cumbrian Words and Phrases*, London.

Dixon P, 1971 Paddock Hole. A Cumberland house with a lower end parlour, in *Transactions of the Cumberland and Westmorland Antiquarian and Archaeological* Society, ns **71**.

Ellwood T ed, 1904 *Anderson's Cumberland Ballads and Songs*. This includes Anderson's poem, 'The Clay Daubin'.

Gate J, 1894 *The History and Topography of Wigton and District*.

Harrison J R, 1989 Some clay dabbins in Cumberland, Part I, in *Transactions of the Ancient Monuments Society*, **33**, 97–151.

Harrison J R, 1991 Some clay dabbins in Cumberland, Part II, in *Transactions of the Ancient Monuments Society*, **35**, 29–88.

Hodgson K S, Bouch C M L and Bulman C G, 1953 Lamonby Farm: a clay house at Burgh by Sands, *Trans. Cumberland and Westmorland Antiquarian And Archaeological Society*, ns **53**.

Howard R et al, 1997 Nottingham University Tree Ring Dating Laboratory: Dendrochronological Survey of Clay Dabbings on the Solway Plain, in *Vernacular Architecture*, **28**, 33–134.

Hutchinson W, 1794 *The History of the County of Cumberland*.

Jennings N, 1993 The buildings of Moorhouse, Burgh by Sands, in *Trans. Cumberland and Westmorland Antiquarian And Archaeological Society* ns **93**.

Jennings N, 1997 Two remarkable Cumbrian clay dabbins, in *Trans. Cumberland and Westmorland Antiquarian And Archaeological Society* ns **97**.

Mercer R, 1997 *Kirkpatrick Fleming, Dumfriesshire: An Anatomy of a Parish in South West Scotland*, Dumfries, Dumfriesshire and Galloway Natural History and Antiquarian Society, 106.

Sinclair, Sir J, 1792 *The First Statistical Account of Scotland*, **2**.

Stell G, 1972 Two cruck-framed buildings in Dumfriesshire, in *Transactions of the Dumfriesshire and Galloway Natural History and Antiquarian Society*, **49**.

Walker B and McGregor C, 1996 *Earth Structures and Construction in Scotland, Historic Scotland* Technical Advice Note **6**, Edinburgh, Historic Scotland.

THE EAST MIDLANDS

Barley M, 1987 *English Farmhouse and Cottage*, Gloucester, Sutton.

Brunskill, R W, 2000, An *Illustrated Handbook of Vernacular Architecture*, London, Faber and Faber.

Cousins R, forthcoming, *Lincolnshire Building in the Mud and Stud Tradition*, Heritage Lincolnshire.

Gorden F, 1998 *Mud and Stud*, unpublished MA dissertation, Institute of Advanced Architectural Studies, York.

Hurd J, 1995 Mud and stud, in *Lincolnshire Life*, June 1996.

Pevsner N and Harris J, 1985 *The Buildings of England: Lincolnshire*, London, Penguin.

SCOTLAND

Fenton A, 1968 Alternating stone and turf – an obsolete building practice, in *Folklife* 6, 94–103.

Fenton A, 1970 Clay building and clay thatch in Scotland, in *Ulster Folklife* 15:16, 28–40.

Fenton A and Walker B, 1981 *The Rural Architecture of Scotland*, Edinburgh, John Donald.

Gailey R A, 1960 The use of mud in thatching in Scotland, in *Ulster Folklife*, **6**, 68–70.

Gardenstone, Lord 1795 *Travelling Memorandums*, Edinburgh, 129–130 (German earth-building technique introduced into Scotland).

Keay J and Keay J 1994, *The Collins Encyclopedia of Scotland*, London, Collins.

Mackenzie W M, 1934 Clay castle-building in Scotland, in *Proceedings of the Society of Antiquaries of Scotland*, **LXVIII**.

Megaw B R S, 1962 The 'moss-houses' of Kincardine, Perthshire, in *Scottish Studies*, **6**, 87–93.

Myles R and Walker B, (forthcoming) *Cottown: A Scottish Mudwall Structure*, Edinburgh, Historic Scotland (Case Study).

Noble R R, 1984 Turf walled houses of the Central Highlands: An experiment in reconstruction, in *Folk-Life*, **22**.

Stephens H and Burn R S, 1861 Pisé, in *Book of Farm Buildings*, 276–281.

Walker B, 1977 *Clay Buildings in North East Scotland*, Dundee and Edinburgh, Scottish Vernacular Buildings Working Group.

Walker B, 1981: Rait, Perthshire, Scotland: An exploration in architectural archaeology, in *Permanent European Conference for the Study of the Rural Landscape: Collected Papers, Denmark, Session 1979*, Copenhagen, 201–211.

Walker B and McGregor C, 1995 A late eighteenth century use of clay in the construction of nine temporary dwellings at Stein, Isle of Skye, Inverness-shire, in *ICOMOS UK: Earth Structures Committee Newsletter*, **III**, 9–11.

Walker B, McGregor C and Stark G, 1996 *Technical Advice Note No. 4 Thatch and Thatching: A Guide to Conserving Scottish Thatching Traditions*, Edinburgh, Historic Scotland.

Walker B and McGregor C, 1996 *Technical Advice Note No. 5 The Hebridean Blackhouse: A Guide to Materials, Construction and Maintenance*, Edinburgh, Historic Scotland.

Walker B and McGregor C, in collaboration with Little R, 1996 *Technical Advice Note No. 6 Earth Structures and Construction in Scotland: A Guide to the Recognition and Conservation of Earth Technology in Scottish Buildings*, Edinburgh, Historic Scotland.

Walker B and McGregor C, 1998 Possible antecedents to Scottish earth building practices in the Mediterranean countries, in *Vernacular Building*, **21** 10–24.

EAST ANGLIA

Bouwens D, 1988 Clay lump in South Norfolk: observations and recollections, in *Vernacular Architecture*, **19**, 10–18.

Harrison J R, 1984 The mud wall in England at the close of the vernacular era, in *Transactions of the Ancient Monuments Society*, ns **28**, 155–174.

Harrison R, 1999 *Earth. The Conservation and Repair of Bowhill, Exeter: Working with Cob,* English Heritage Research Transactions and Case Studies in Architectural Conservation, **3**, London, English Heritage.

McCann J, 1995 *Clay and Cob Buildings*, 2nd ed, Princes Risborough, Shire.

McCann J, 1987 Is clay-lump a traditional building material? in *Vernacular Architecture*, **18**, 1–16.

McCann J, 1987 The first cottage of clay bats? In *Proceedings of the Cambridge Antiquarian Society*, **76**, 113–121.

Middleton G F, 1995 *Bulletin 5: Earth Wall Construction and Engineering,* North Ryde, New South Wales.

Norton J, 1997 *Building with Earth: A Handbook,* Rugby, Intermediate Technology Group.

Proctor J M, 1979 *East Anglian Cottages*, Ely, Providence Press.

Wade-Martins P, 1993 *An Historical Atlas of Norfolk*, Norwich, Norfolk Musuems Service.

Walker B, 1977 *Buildings in North East Scotland*, Dundee and Edinburgh, Scottish Vernacular Buildings Working Group.

William-Ellis C, 1999, *Building in Cob, Pisé and Stabilized Earth,* Shaftesbury, Donhead.

WESSEX

Albery J, 1962 *Building in Chalk, Pisé and Cob*, Keystone No 4, 14–15

Handy T, 1982 *Transactions of the Association for Studies in the Conservation of Historic Buildings*, **7**, 69.

James J F, 1977 *Annual Report of the Hampshire Field Club*, Hampshire Field Club, New Forest Section, 20–25.

Nixon B H, 1946 *Journal of the Junior Institution of Engineers,* **56**, 240–243.

Pearson G T, 1984 *Chartered Quantity Surveyor,* Royal Institution of Chartered Surveyors, January, 216.

Pearson G T, 1986 *Traditional Homes Magazine*, June, 30–34.

Pearson G T, 1989 *Celebrating Samborne.* The Samborne and District Society, 44–50.

Pearson G T, 1984 Hampshire's Chalk Heritage, in *Hampshire Magazine*, January, 34–36.

Sumner H, 1923 A Guide to the New Forest, in C Brown.

Vancouver C, 1813 *A General View of the Agriculture of Hampshire*, London, Sherwood, Nealy and Jones.

Whitlock R, 1976 *The Folklore of Wiltshire*, Batsford.

DEVON AND CORNWALL

Devon Earth Building Association, 1993 *Appropriate Plasters, Renders and Finishes for Cob and Random Stone Walls*, Exeter, Devon Earth Building Association.

Devon Earth Building Association, 1997 *Cob and the 1991 Building Regulations*, Exeter, Devon Earth Building Association.

Devon Historic Buildings Trust, 1992 *The Cob Buildings of Devon 1: History, building methods and conservation*, Devon, Devon Historic Buildings Trust.

Devon Historic Buildings Trust, 1993 *The Cob Buildings of Devon 2: Repair and maintenance,* Devon, Devon Historic Buildings Trust.

ARCHAEOLOGY

Allcroft A H, 1908, *Earthwork of England*, London.

Beresford F, 1975 *The Medieval Village: Excavations at Goltho and Barton Blount*, Society for Medieval Archaeology Monograph Series **6**.

Beresford M and St Joseph J K S, 1977 *Medieval England. An Aerial Survey*, Cambridge.

Bowen C, 1961 *Ancient Fields*, British Association for the Advancement of Science.

Clifton-Taylor A, 1972 *The Pattern of English Building*, London, Faber and Faber.

Cocroft W D, forthcoming, *Dangerous Energy: the Archaeology of Gunpowder and Military Explosives Manufacture*, London, English Heritage.

Cook H and Williamson T eds, 1999 *Water Management in the English Landscape. Field, Marsh and Meadow*, Edinburgh.

Darvill T C and Fulton A, 1998, *The Monuments at Risk Survey of England* Devon Earth Building Association, Main Report, Bournemouth University and English Heritage.

Fairclough G, 1999 *Historic Landscape Characterisation*, London, English Heritage.

Fleming A, 1988 *The Dartmoor Reaves*, Batsford.

Frere S S and St Joseph S, 1983, *Roman Britain from the Air*, Cambridge.

Hall D, 1995 *The Open Fields of Northamptonshire*, Northampton Record Society.

Higham R and Barker P, 1992 *Timber Castles*, Batsford.

Maxwell G S ed, 1983 *The Impact of Aerial Reconnaissance on Archaeology*, Council for British Archaeology Research Report 49.

Oswald et al, forthcoming *Neolithic Enclosures*, London, English Heritage.

Palmer R, 1984 *Danebury An Iron Age Hillfort in Hampshire, An Aerial Photographic Interpretation of its Environs*, Royal Commission on the Historic Monuments of England Supplementary Series No. 6.

Roberts B K and Wrathmell, forthcoming *An Atlas of Rural Settlement in England*, London, English Heritage.

Royal Commission on the Historic Monuments of England 1998, *MIDAS. A Manual and Data Standard for Monument Inventories*, Swindon, Royal Commission on the Historic Monuments of England.

Riley D N, 1987 *Air Photography and Archaeology*, London.

Stoertz C, 1997 *Ancient Landscapes of the Yorkshire Wolds: Aerial Photographic Transcription and Analysis*, Swindon.

Wilson D R, 1982 Air Photo *Interpretation for Archaeologists*, Batsford.

WORLD HERITAGE SITES

International Council of Monuments and Sites 1966 *International Charter for the Conservation and restoration of Monuments and Sites*, re-issue of the 'Venice Charter' of 1964, (text in English, Spanish, French and Russian), Paris, ICOMOS.

International Council of Monuments and Sites 1974 *Manuel des Legislazion Nationales, le Protection du Patrimoine Cultural* (Manual of national legislation on the protection of cultural property), Paris, ICOMOS.

International Council of Monuments and Sites 1979 *The Australia ICOMOS Charter for the Conservation of Places*, adopted at the Australia ICOMOS meeting at Burra, S.A., 18 August, 1979, Canberra, ICOMOS.

BRITISH EARTH BUILDING IN THE NEW MILLENNIUM

Harries W J R and Clark D, 1996 *An Investigation of an 'Aggregate-claystone' Mix from Cadeby Quarry, Doncaster as a Material for Rammed Earth Construction*. Unpublished report at Centre for Earthen Architecture (CEA), University of Plymouth.

Devon Earth Building Association, 1996 *Cob and the Building Regulations*, Exeter, Devon Earth Building Association.

Ford M, in preparation, The Development of a Methodology for Creating an Earthen Building Inventory. Unpublished PhD thesis, Centre for Earthen Architecture (CEA), University of Plymouth.

Houben H, 1995, Earthen Architecture and Modernity, in *Out of Earth II*, Watson L and Harries WJR, eds, conference proceedings, University of Plymouth.

Minke G, 1994 The Building Material Earth: its properties and possibilities to refine them, in *Out of Earth*, Watson L and Harding S, eds, conference proceedings, University of Plymouth.

Wimmel B, 1995 *Prima Materia – the earth building material rediscovered*, video by Nord Film Produktionsgemeinschaft.